July 18, 1990.

To Charles -
   This looks like an
account you might enjoy.
   Love,
        Mother

        Another book!

LONDON PARTICULARS

C. H. ROLPH

LONDON
PARTICULARS

Oxford New York Toronto Melbourne
OXFORD UNIVERSITY PRESS
1980

Oxford University Press, Walton Street, Oxford OX2 6DP

OXFORD LONDON GLASGOW
NEW YORK TORONTO MELBOURNE WELLINGTON
KUALA LUMPUR SINGAPORE JAKARTA HONG KONG TOKYO
DELHI BOMBAY CALCUTTA MADRAS KARACHI
NAIROBI DAR ES SALAAM CAPE TOWN

© *C.H. Rolph 1980*

British Library Cataloguing in Publication Data

Rolph, C.H.
London particulars.
1. London — Social life and customs
I. Title
942.1'083'0924   *DA688*   79-41639
ISBN 0-19-211755-6

*Printed in Great Britain by
Lowe & Brydone (Printers) Ltd.,
Thetford, Norfolk*

CONTENTS

FOREWORD

'C. H. Rolph' has been a pen-name since 1924, and was constructed by shifting around the names in Cecil Rolph Hewitt
(these appear on my birth certificate) so as to conceal my
identity at a time when the concealment seemed prudent. It
may be necessary to explain this in launching a bookful of
Hewitts. After about 1946, when I went to work on the *New
Statesman*, I became known as Bill (to almost everyone) because Kingsley Martin thought the other names were absurd
and was prone to rechristen people. But in the days of Edward
VII I was known as Cecil at home and Suet at school, and re-
collect neither with the smallest pleasure.

C. H. R.

1

SOUTHWARK

There were times when my carefully respectable father would tell me, more than half meaning it, that I was a guttersnipe. By the time I was old enough to read, I was old enough also to feel that this might be something to be resented. Above all, I was old enough to use a dictionary, a practice (some would have called ours an obsession) with which he infected me as soon as I could read. It was thus that I learned I was a street urchin. Given a good beginning, my father said, in a Christian household (more usually my mother's phrase), I was from choice living as a street urchin, with other urchins as my boon companions. I knew only too well that he was sometimes rather ashamed of me. When I was older I heard him describe Lloyd George as a guttersnipe. I never knew why, though it may have meant that the Welsh Wizard was a womanizing pro-Boer; also Keir Hardie, probably for wearing a cloth cap to the Palace of Westminster when he had been elected; and T. E. Dunville for being a smutty comedian —whom, of course, I accordingly longed to hear. But he had allowed me, as soon as I was considered old enough—and I shall never forget the day—to play in the street because there was nowhere else within a reasonable distance where children could communally play. And playing in the street is, I suppose, one of the many themes of this book.

Until I was eighteen months old I lived in my birthplace, No. 28 Ilfracombe Buildings, Marshalsea Road, Southwark. Insalubrious, my father always called it in later years. I do not pretend to have had, at that age, any developed ideas about salubriousness. In matters of early memory I willingly yield the palm to the Emperor Caligula, who claimed to recall the admiration on the midwives' faces as they washed him after his emergence into the waiting Roman world. But Ilfracombe Buildings, now

Ilfracombe Flats, was and is surrounded by little thoroughfares with names like Quilp Street, Copperfield Street, Weller Road, Pickwick Street, and Little Dorrit Court, all reflecting the fact that Dickens's parents had spent some months in the Marshalsea Prison while he, as a blacking-factory boy, was accommodated in nearby Lant Street. (They were in the prison from February to May 1824 for a debt of £10, a sum which had always been enough to keep a friendless debtor in there until he died.) But Dickens died in 1870, and the Dickensian names were not bestowed on Southwark streets and passages for years to come. (Shall we, in due course, see a James Bond Court, a Maigret Mews, a Morecambe and Wise Passage?) I shall construct no fanciful links between my adult involvement in prison reform, dating from about 1940, and the fact that I was born where a horrible prison once stood, a prison with far too cosy a reputation to match its ghastly history. It was closed in 1842; the end, according to a contemporary broadsheet, of 'a very hell upon earth' for those without money for propitiating gaolers.

If a city can be said to have a spirit, a benign spirit of London had nevertheless saturated those precincts. And I came to call myself a Cockney with a pride that might not have survived any real investigation of that word's much-disputed etymology. The meaning I chose, of course, was the one about being born within sound (as I certainly was) of the great bell of the Church of St. Mary-le-Bow, Cheapside. I didn't get to know the older meanings—milksop, town-bred softie and so on—for many years. I soon learned, though, that the benign spirit recognized in those parts was that of Mr George Foster Peabody, the American grocer-philanthropist who, leaving his native Massachusetts in 1837 to come and live in England, gave half a million pounds to the London poor and his name to a number of housing estates and 'artisans' dwellings'. Of these, Ilfracombe Buildings was one. My father, who was a police sergeant when I was born, thought we were a cut above artisans. I think we were a cut below.

The first 'Peabody Buildings', opened in Spitalfields in 1864, had been vicariously appreciated by the rich and eagerly sought after by the poor. But since that time a Peabody Estate had become the kind of address which (if you had it) you pretended not to have; and I recall that my elder brother Harold and I felt at one time that a Peabody Estate was little better, in any social sense, than the Marshalsea Prison itself. I suppose therefore that we were the happier for not knowing that our parents were the tenants and beneficiaries of the admirable Mr Peabody, so that we were able to feel sorry for other children who lived in named and identifiable Peabody structures. Strange that Mr Peabody, Lord Rowton, Dr Barnardo and similar patrons should always provoke a petty bourgeois reaction of this kind. It is the fashion nowadays to regard the Peabody Buildings as the planners' opening attack on the established neighbourliness of the slums. They did not succeed in killing neighbourliness at once because they were not allowed to build high enough. You need about twenty floors.

But it was because of Mr Peabody that we were able to inhabit a clean, bug-free, well-lighted and commodious flat for six shillings a week. How odd that we should all feel a bit proud that we had lived on the actual site of a ghastly prison. I suppose its disappearance had taken place long enough ago for it to be spoken of with the historical detachment some of us seem able to feel about the Games of the Romans, their mass crucifixion of slaves to provide a street decoration in honour of visiting potentates, and all the other atrocities by which the Roman name is so strangely unsullied.

Once at least during the Marshalsea period I fell down one of the short flights of stone stairs by which the residents spirally approached their front doors (as indeed they still do). This was before I was able to walk—which, I am told, I did at thirteen months, though my brother Harold's grudging confirmation of this achievement always described it as an ungainly waddle which I never outgrew. I can't remember whether I was hurt or injured in the fall: probably not, since babies have a rubber-like composition, but I feel certain that it was this experience which left me with a secret terror of stairs that burdens me to this day. Going down a long flight with no hand-rail (no trouble about going up) induces in me an almost insane single-mindedness and, even in the liveliest company, a tense inability to converse. And although I can go up them two at a time, I must now disclose for the first time that going down two at a time is simply not to be thought of, an accomplishment in others which I have watched with miserable envy all my life. There came a point, in the thirties, when I had nearly brought myself to do it, experimentally, on the stairs at the Bank Underground Station; and it was then, of course, that I had to begin wearing bifocal glasses. Once you do that, any kind of derring-do on staircases belongs to the past.

There was an eight-year-old resident at Ilfracombe Buildings, named Frankie Pink, who could jump down each flight of stairs in one go by holding on to the handrails. Even Harold (and my cousin Herbert from the flat below, of whom more anon) had to regard this with passive admiration, investing Frankie Pink with the necessary authority enabling him to take them both daily to school.

There is a lot to be said about stairs, possibly a whole book to be written about them, taking in Clovelly, Paris, the Alpine villages and the Acropolis. Think of the detached architectural view of the human race which can build tower-blocks for it to live in, and equip them with lifts whose frequent breakdown can be foreseen by anyone who is not an architect; rather as a boy will construct obstacles in a small cage to provide fun and exercise for his resentful white mice. Think of the mysterious behaviour of escalator handrails, which move at a different speed from the stairs and seem either to stretch your arm to twice its length or telescope it into your shoulder; of the huge difference, in terms of human effort and fatigue, between six-inch and eight-inch 'risers'; and of what all this does to the developing mind of a child.

The fact that at this stage I still preferred crawling to walking meant that my poor mother, lacking not only a pushchair but (I must suppose) the means to buy one, carried me in her arms everywhere when she had to take me out. I made this worse by being an outsize baby, and I recall with embarrassment rather than pride the fact—or rather the unanimous family accusation

—that I weighed 12½ lb on arrival. I do not see how one can refute this kind of thing. Both my mother and her sister (my Aunt Carrie, who was later to become my stepmother), became permanently and rather horribly round-shouldered from their early teens, because of this baby-carrying business. And it must have been when thus carried that I first saw the masts of the ships moored eastward of London Bridge, without of course knowing what they were. It is this recollection, and the fact that I later thought they must have been trees growing on the tops of houses, which demonstrates (of course to myself alone) that it is possible to think before you have acquired any vocabulary; possible, that is to say, to distinguish between various objects seen and registered namelessly in the memory. I can also remember that my rattle, of which I was in no way ashamed and which must therefore have had the approval normal among people of my age, was in fact a tin, probably a cocoa-tin, containing pebbles; and that I identified these pebbles with the ones to be seen in window boxes and hurled into the street below. Harold once took the lid off my tin to show me what made the noise, and I was furious that no one else would ever show me again, probably because it was supposed that I should be fool enough to swallow the pebbles.

I once had the pleasure, I think it was in the late fifties, of interviewing Sir Julian Huxley in one of a series of BBC radio programmes called *Frankly Speaking*. Before it began we had a meal with the producer and somebody else, and I got Sir Julian to talk about H. G. Wells, one of his closest friends and one of my pagan gods. He expressed surprise that Wells had not been able to remember his own childhood before about the age of six, whereas his own recollections began at four. Indeed in his autobiographical *Memories* he says, 'my first conscious memory dates from when I was four', and it was when his nurse took him for a walk at Charterhouse Green and a fat toad hopped out of a hawthorn hedge in front of them. 'What a creature,' he wrote, 'with its warty skin, its big eyes bulging up, and its awkward movements. That comic toad helped to determine my career as a scientific naturalist.' He told me that he didn't see how memory could possibly pre-date speech and the capacity to name things; and in the presence of so renowned a thinker I could only be silent but confused.

I have to admit that *very* early memories can be faulty, misleading, and conducive in later years to defensive rationalization. Many times as a child I protested in tears, for instance, that I had *really* seen steam trains going across London Bridge, when everyone assured me that it had never happened. London Bridge, pronounced my father when he was eventually drawn into the controversy, was *not* a railway bridge. But what I had seen was, I now have no doubt, Foden-type traction engines puffing over the bridge to Leadenhall Market, great clanging masses of whirling machinery on iron-shod wheels. At twelve months I had no conceivable means of mentally recording these in any verbal terms, but recorded them nonetheless; possibly because at that time all traffic was horse-drawn and the sight of a 'locomotive' was a nine days' wonder that would have brought excited exclamations from the grown-ups, including the one carrying me.

It must have been within a few months of these London Bridge episodes that we moved to 101 Woodstock Road, Finsbury Park; and since the rear windows of that house looked out on to the Great Northern Railway I could thenceforth report the passage of steam engines without fear of derision.

I have always been slightly surprised that from that period I have absolutely no recollection of food or drink. I was not a breast-fed baby (I don't know why) and, as so many infants were in those days, I was 'reared' on diluted Nestlé's Milk from a feeding bottle. Much more interesting (to me) is that although I cannot remember either of my parents from that time, I do vaguely remember two adult figures whom I came to love and respect with a special kind of devotion. One was my Aunt Florrie, who lived in the flat underneath ours at Marshalsea Road. The other, strangely, was my 'Cousin' Florrie (truly no cousin at all—her mother was a cousin by marriage of one of my grandfathers); a vivid, loving, laughing, opinionated woman, an unmarried school-teacher of the kind who knew Scott,

Dickens, Jane Austen and all the Brontës backwards and went to the Holy Land for carefully financed holidays, and who took a special interest in me as (I'm told) 'the deep one'. But I have satisfied myself that my memory of them begins in 1902 and just before my first birthday. Of that period they are the only two people, of whatever age, whom I can remember. What I didn't know for many years was that my father tolerated Cousin Florrie affectionately as a 'crackpot', and that this may have had something to do with the fact that she sternly disapproved of my Nestlé's Milk diet and foretold that its consequences would be dire. I have never really felt like a dire consequence, but I have always liked condensed milk and have resented, throughout a long life, the need for this attachment to remain furtive. One biographical detail endlessly and mercilessly recalled by elders and betters is that I once poured the whole contents of a freshly-opened tin on to the tray of my high chair, dabbled my palms in it, and orgiastically spread it over my face. I have always denied it.

I believe, however, that I may be unusual in recalling, as a pocket-sized surge of emotion, the scorn with which I observed other infants in high prams, boat-shaped and hooded things on four big wheels which were then properly called bassinets or perambulators (sometimes both, anyway in the advertisements) and have since come to be known, under American influence, as baby carriages. Today I have friends, of my own considerable age, who remember their prams and recall particularly the taste of the leather strap that kept them in, which it was usual to suck as a means of passing the time. But I myself never rode in one of these, and I am sure that in my own infancy we never had such a thing in the family. When I began consciously observing the world about me, people of my age had been sharply divided into three classes: those who lay down in high prams, pulling themselves up (when they could) to look over the sides; those who sat, or lolled sideways, in 'go-carts'; and those, like me, who had to be carried everywhere until they could walk. This is the earliest, and the most poignant, of all the great class distinctions.

Go-carts were little folding contraptions (pinching many a finger) with a kind of limp mackintosh seat and with four very small metal-rimmed wheels. There was no such thing in our household then, though I occasionally rode in other people's. By this time we had moved to Finsbury Park. Here a neighbour of ours called Wally Gerrard, my senior by seven months, commonly rode in one of these things, and when I was taken to see him I spent the whole of each visit pushing his go-cart up and down a narrow corridor leading from his front door to the back of the house. I think there was probably room to turn it round at the end of each unsteady journey, but it was easier to work your way round the go-cart, even if you had to sit down heavily once or twice in the process, and then simply put the vehicle into reverse. So it was in fact with someone else's go-cart that I learned to walk.

I believe this was usual enough, but my parents had the wisdom to ensure that I did it only indoors and, so far as possible, on one level. Another neighbour called Elaine Phipps, who could (I grudgingly concede) walk rather better than I at that period although a mere six weeks my senior, pushed Wally Gerrard's go-cart down some area steps and followed it down before she realized what they were. It was some time before we met again. And I think this is the point where I refute some reflections about the ground-floor passages in London terrace houses of the early nineteen-hundreds.

Halfway through each house, from front to back, they all had a single step down, the bane of mothers carrying babies or trays, and of arthritic old ladies. Until the age of 15, in Finsbury Park and Fulham, I lived in and visited an assortment of such houses and in this respect they were all the same. A passage went straight through from front door to back kitchen, but halfway along there was this single step down. After about the age of eighteen months I found this mid-passage step a useful point of practice in the important accomplishment of getting down and up at kerbstones without actually stopping to, so to speak, arrange oneself. Older boys and girls, coming across a road, could do this running, let alone walking. For many months

I had secretly supposed that, alone of my kind, I should always have to pause at every step-up or kerbstone, turn sideways, and then climb up like a crab. Long afterwards my father recalled how, at that stage, I was always falling down at this precise spot in other people's passages. I was practising, preparing myself for the outer world of streets and pavements.

The time came, once this single step down had completed my training and was thus of no further use, when I cursed it as an architectural blunder of the first magnitude. What was the use of it? Any go-cart would pitch over as soon as you got there, whereupon it was necessary to summon attendants to get it righted. You completed the journey to the kitchen door and back again; and there you were, trapped once again. Any attempt to push the thing up the step meant that you sat down heavily again, the go-cart falling this time on top of you, and the attendants had to be brought back more stridently than before. It was some years before I became aware of a theory of my father's, which was that these little houses retained their two ground-floor levels as a vestigial reminder of the upstairs-downstairs complex. The front parlour, he said, where you had tea on Sundays, was still actually as well as notionally 'upstairs', a place to which underlings could be summoned by bells. It was as snobbish and stupid as the use of 'Esquire' in addressing letters to ordinary people like ourselves. But my elder brother Harold liked it, and liked the notion of having a scullery that went with it. 'Away, you scullion,' he would later say to me, fresh from his homework on *Henry IV Part 2*, 'and skulk into the scullery.'

Much later I learned from builders that it was all due to damp. At the back of the house were the kitchen and scullery, which needed stone floors because of washing day and cookery. But stone floors for the front rooms would have been, in those days, unthinkable. You needed wooden floor-boards, or thought you did, on which to lay and fasten your linoleum or (occasionally) carpeting. And boards, if you must have them, had to be protected from damp by being raised sufficiently to allow for a series of air-bricks round the periphery. Now that people don't

mind concrete floors front and back, or get them whether they
mind or not, there is no longer any need for the different floor
levels; and pushing a go-cart through these modern houses must
be wonderful. It may not, I suppose, be so character-forming.

Southwark, originally a Roman settlement, became London's
South Wark, work, werke, or fortification; and in 982 had been
under Danish siege for nearly a century. When the Londoners
finally gave in to Canute in 1017 it was called Suthgeweorke,
'South fortified place'. It seems to have been the fate of fortified places to be regularly destroyed and rebuilt, and Southwark
was utterly destroyed times without number. The efforts of the
German air force in two world wars were laughable by comparison with the destructive genius of William the Conqueror and
the incendiaries who had preceded him down the centuries.
The repeated obliteration of Southwark, indeed of London, by
foreign forces had become part of my own historical stock-in-
trade by the time I came to learn, through the bewildering
lines from *King John*, that English history and Shakespeare
were not the same thing:

> This England never did, nor never shall
> Lie at the proud foot of a conqueror.

This England, however, lay always open to limited conquest
at the hands of any inquisitive and thrusting child who, like
myself, was determined to enjoy the simpler things in life. It
was with the move to Finsbury Park in 1903 that the process
began to take shape. My mother told me much later that all
our furniture went to Finsbury Park on a greengrocer's cart,
never dispelling the confused picture I thus acquired of beds,
cupboards, chairs, and tables piled among cabbages, potatoes,
and carrots on a little cart drawn by a straining pony. Moreover the greengrocer's cart got lost for hours in the worst
'pea soup' fog that my parents ever remembered, a yellow, acrid
smothering fog of the kind then known as a London Particular,
a fog such as darkens the opening pages of *Bleak House*. ('I
asked him whether there was a great fire anywhere, for the
streets were so full of dense brown smoke that scarcely anything

was to be seen. "Oh dear no miss," he said. "This is a London particular." I had never heard of such a thing. "A fog miss," said the young gentleman. "Oh indeed," said I.') The greengrocer and his mate, before they left us that morning with all our possessions on their cart, tied big handkerchiefs around their mouths and noses; and I was not taken down into the darkening street to see them go. In later years I groped my way to school in many a London Particular. I always found them frightening though not, so far as I was concerned, injurious; but I now know that they caused many deaths and I have never understood why Londoners seemed always to speak of them with proud proprietorship. But the fact that the job was done (as so much removals work was then done) by a greengrocer is fixed in my mind by my mother's further information that inside this greengrocer's shop was a chalked notice saying 'Move with us by Moonlight!'

It must have been a legacy from the days when, as Dickens said of his parents' home in Lant Street, Southwark (which is still one of the boundaries of the Peabody Estate), 'local inhabitants were migratory, disappearing usually towards the verge of quarter-day'. The misfortunes of Dickens's father, by the way, may well have encouraged the settled formation of the Civil Service in the 1850s; for though the migrations of Dickens senior, from Portsea to London and then to Chatham, were the outcome of his job as clerk in the Navy Pay Office, he was always in the kind of money difficulties specially unsuitable in that kind of job, difficulties which the security of the Civil Service seems largely to have banished from the lives of its members; and from which, because of my own father's job, my childhood was mercifully free.

2

FINSBURY PARK

This is not a story of poverty; many autobiographers who are not rich, and even some who are, have seemed eager to talk of hungry beginnings. We were never poor. My father's police pay at the time of my birth was 28 shillings a week. You couldn't buy much with that, but if a family breadwinner confined himself to the winning of bread, and (like both my parents) was a non-smoker and teetotaller, his children could have shoes on their feet, adequate if makeshift clothes on their bodies, an occasional hair-cut, and reasonably distended bellies. At the time of which I am writing, Charlie Chaplin (who died worth untold millions) was living a London life of real poverty, including two long sessions with his brother Syd in the kind of workhouse which ruthlessly separated children from their mothers within the same building. Chaplin's *Autobiography*, describing the Walworth, Newington, and Southwark area exactly as it still was when I was born, tells of his early years with a detachment and acceptance astounding in a man so conditioned by a long lifetime of show business to be sentimental and histrionic. I knew and played with urchins of the kind he there remembers: not in Southwark, where I was only a baby, but in Finsbury Park and Fulham; where, no doubt, I could have played with boys from rather more genteel families but preferred not to. Kingsley Amis, who was later a boy in Streatham and Norbury, calls that 'a lower middle class area, which meant that you had to be very careful not to slip into the working class'. I suppose I was a bit lower down in the same stratum, but not nearly careful enough. My street companions were a constant source of disapproval among the family; worrying my father, puzzling my mother, and provoking in my elder brother Harold, who went to better schools, a profound distaste which he was never slow to display or even to express.

We had arrived at No. 101 Woodstock Road, a narrow terrace house of three storeys whose front windows overlooked (and still do) the playground of a huge primary school, while the rear windows and the tiny back garden looked on to the main railway line from London to the North. And on the far side of that lies the splendid acreage of Finsbury Park itself. In 1978, after an interval of exactly 75 years, I went back on a spring evening to re-examine this unhallowed spot, and to find the house looking as though, in three-quarters of a century, it had had no lick or smell of paint, and that strips of matchboarding had been used instead of glass to repair the windows as they got broken or fell out. It might have been a rooming-house in Spanish Harlem. I would have concluded, indeed, that the whole decrepit length of Woodstock Road had fallen victim to 'planning blight' but for the fact that a dozen or more of its houses were then being gutted for reconstruction, their entrails lying bleakly in the roadway in heaps or crammed into builders' skips. Many of the little front 'gardens' had been concreted over to accommodate elderly motor vehicles whose outlines were picked out in brown rust; and in the roadway, which in my infancy was a teeming playground safe from traffic, there wasn't a child to be seen. The few I did see, idling on corners, sitting on low walls or playing leapfrog on the pavements, seemed to be nearly all black, happy-looking and well-dressed.

Woodstock Road School, where the Middlesex County Council was to launch me on the ocean of education at the age of three, is now called Stroud Green First School and looks much the same as I remember it; enormous and forbidding in appearance, a place of which, even if Heaven lay about us in our classified infancy, you could have confidently said that shades of the prison house were already closing upon the growing boy. Finsbury Park, by the way, is a part of Hornsey, which for rather boring historical reasons has never been part of the area educated by the London County Council or (now) the Greater London Council. But the school in my time had a teacher, a Miss Hyte (Hite, Height, or Heit), a thin little woman whose face I completely forget except for her steel-rimmed spectacles, who taught me to read in a few months. I don't think she could have known how I was getting on, for she had a class of about fifty to instruct in all subjects. On Friday afternoons we were reading 'round the class' a mercifully abridged and simplified version of *The Water Babies*. (I can see it now, with its limp blue covers, probably buckram, its large print, and its lovely 'straight' illustrations—the people who drew the pictures for children's books had not yet decided that their readers wanted distorted and hideous grotesques.) At these illustrations you could contentedly gaze all the time if you were one of the majority not yet able to read and not trying to. It was only those able to read who dared to stand up when their turn came: illiterates like myself sat still and wondered when they might have the effrontery to stand up and have a go as Miss Hyte's gentle voice said 'N-n-n-next?' I was reminded of all this when, at the age of about twelve, I came to read George Moore's *Esther Waters* and to weep secretly when poor Esther breaks down on being required to read from the Bible. It happens at a Sunday afternoon gathering of the domestic staff in their mistress's drawing-room, and they too are 'reading round the class' as we did. 'You can't read, can you Esther?' says the surprised mistress kindly. And Esther sobs.

Suddenly one Friday *The Water Babies* came alive for me. I saw what all these clever and older children were up to. Having puzzled out three or four words in advance of what was being read aloud, you could then, instead of grinding out one lonely word at a time, with pauses for encouragement between each, release them in a more or less unbroken stream, like paying out a coil of rope as you went along. It was an intoxicating, almost a stupefying discovery. My brother Roland, five years my junior, had a very similar experience at his Fulham school years later, and told me the feeling was akin to a sudden ability to fly; and he remembers, as I do not, a disappointingly inadequate response when he brought the news home after school. In my case, instead of sitting silent as usual when my opportunity came, I got up. I can remember reading the phrase

'His mother was detter-mind' when Miss Hyte stopped me. 'Do that one again?' she said. I mumbled for a bit. 'Detter-mind' I muttered again, defiantly. 'Oh—*determined*', I shrieked excitedly, and she laughed with glee. Did I know what it meant, she asked? I plainly didn't. I had doubtless heard the word often at home, for my father was always being determined about something. She told us all the meaning of determined, adding that all of us could read if we were determined to read. Never have I felt such inflation; never, I hope and believe, been such a prig.

The priggishness was short-lived. Within a few weeks Miss Hyte had me out in front of the class on Friday afternoons, as one of a trio reading out stories about the Labours of Hercules: the other two readers were girls much older than I, they gave themselves airs, and to me the whole arrangement quickly became highly embarrassing. Its only advantage was that for ten minutes or so it got me nearer to the fire, the only source of warmth in a big classroom. (None of us seemed to mind the cold very much—I can't recall any grumbling, though there were many chilblains.) I came to dread Fridays, my impresario saw that I did, and after a month or two she let me off. But on that Friday with *The Water Babies* I had pushed open a magic casement. Reading had begun, life had begun. 'People say that life is the thing,' wrote Logan Pearsall Smith (he was to become one of my heroes), 'but I prefer reading.' So did I. And it was lucky for me that mine was a reading family, my father the most avid reader of us all. By some standards, of course, I was a very late starter. In his Introduction to the *Journals of Arnold Bennett*, Mr Frank Swinnerton mentions that Bennett 'remembered pretending to read' at the age of three, but Compton Mackenzie had 'taught himself to read before he was two', while his mother and her sister Isabel had read Rollins's long Roman history before they were two and a half, his mother's favourite book at the age of four being Laurence Sterne's *Sentimental Journey*. No? Well, it's in Octave One (1883–1891) of his autobiography *My Life and Times*, and you must decide for yourself.

I am not able to say with certainty that I remember my first unscripted and unrehearsed speech, and I allow in my own mind for the probability that I merely remember what I have been told I said. Yet I clearly recall the occasion itself, and have been able to establish it as taking place when I was aged two years and nine months. A very large policeman came to our front door at Woodstock Road, a Metropolitan Policeman entrusted with a message telephoned from the City Police. It was (I gather) about a change in my father's duties. I had recently mastered the overhead skill of opening doors but had never before, I believe, had an opportunity to open the front door to the street. This was secured by a safety chain permitting an aperture of about three inches. The eyes of the policeman on the doorstep followed the aperture down until he saw the size of his colloquist. He stooped and put his hands on his knees.

'Daddy or Mummy in?' he said through the small opening.

There was none of this daddy and mummy nonsense in our house. These were baby noises.

'Father's in the lavatory and Mother's bathing', I said tersely.

I have never been allowed to forget this, and learned to support its repeated narration throughout my childhood and adolescence with the sickly complaisance that only the growing child and the adolescent can really understand. Incidentally it must have been at about this time that we had stopped calling my parents Mama and Papa. Harold, then nearly six, announced that it was soppy and made other boys laugh. My father seems to have had no strong feeling about it, but said it was thus that he had always addressed his own parents. This ought to have been enough for us: Grandfather Hewitt, whom we had never known, we had always thought of as a Great Soldier—he was killed at Isandhlwana in the Zulu War in 1879 and was therefore a hero. But my father explained years later that 'Papa' originally meant the Pope, and he wasn't much attached to it. So he became 'Father', and the babyish Mama was superseded too. Daddy and Mummy they had never been.

It was at about this time too that I wanted to learn knitting and crochet, and (I am surprised now to reflect) knew the difference between them, or anyway knew that crochet needed a hook and knitting did not. The reason for this unusual appetite seems to me worth recording.

Electric light was still unknown in ordinary houses—and even our big school was gaslit. Therefore a used electric light bulb was a rare sight among us; indeed among the older boys at school it was worth six cigarette cards at the rate of exchange then prevailing. Now my Cousin Florrie, of whom I have already told you, was a constant visitor at our house, often bringing with her a young fellow-teacher named Cissie Coney (whom she always called 'Cone') to make up a four with my parents at Bezique. One day Miss Coney produced an electric light bulb encased in a crochet cover from which there hung down a thimble, also covered in crochet to look like a basket. At that time there was in progress a national revival of ballooning as a sport (it was actually more than a century old), fostered by the founding of the Royal Aero Club in 1901. Everyone was balloon mad. From about 1903 onwards the catch-phrase 'What time does the balloon go up?' was a common form of enquiry about the start of literally anything. On a real balloon, the usual method of supporting the passenger-carrying basket was to attach it to a net which covered the entire envelope. Miss Coney had discovered that if she transformed electric light bulbs into little model balloons in this way she could sell them to novelty shops; and accordingly, I'm told, this strange occupation began to fill her leisure hours to the exclusion of all else.

I have two good reasons for remembering Miss Coney. First, she gave me one of these balloons for my fourth birthday, and it was one of the very first new toys I ever had. Second, on one of her earlier visits, anxious to demonstrate to her not merely that I could now stand on my own two feet but could stand on my hands with my feet against the wall, I took up this position in the sitting-room and issued the confident challenge, 'Look quick, Cone, could you do this Cone?' Everyone assures me that the challenge was neither taken up nor appreciated by the rather prim Miss Coney, and that I had to be apologized for.

I most earnestly wanted to go to school. The school play-ground was just across the road from the house we lived in, and from the first-floor windows its occupants' behaviour could be studied during the manic fifteen minutes before lessons, morning and afternoon. Other shows took place during the two periods which are known as playtime but which to the outsider looked exactly the same. Each of these frantic and ear-splitting episodes came to an end at the ringing of a handbell; not abruptly, but by a fairly swift diminuendo, like an echo dying away. And then the playground stood empty, a desert of asphalt. Once the children had all disappeared, I had very little idea as to what they did inside the huge building. I probably supposed they were resting in order to gain strength for the next outburst of open-air riot.

But I had some months in which to study all this, and my own position in relation to it. I have been told that not a day passed without my begging, sometimes in tears, to be allowed to go across to the school. It was lucky for my frustrated scholarship that I did not know at the time, but there were younger people than I already there—I have mentioned that there were a few scholars of two and a half. It was lucky also that I didn't know how the law stood concerning compulsory school attendance, and that it would be a further two and a half years before I could claim to go as a matter of right. I have recently looked at the Rules and Regulations made in 1903 by the Borough of Hornsey Education Committee 'For the Management of the Schools Maintained by the Town Council' —of which Woodstock Road School was one. They ordain that no child between three and fifteen whose parents lived in the Borough could be refused admission 'so long as there is room for it'. The school hours were from 9 till 12 and from 2 till 4.30, except that *infants* could leave at 4 o'clock during the winter. For misconduct we could be 'kept in' after hours, but not for more than 30 minutes; and for backwardness or dull-ness we could not be punished at all (at subsequent schools those were, in fact, the only things I was ever punished for). Corporal punishment could be administered *only* by the head teacher. And my marvellous woman teacher with the steel-rimmed glasses would, I find, have been lucky to be earning £68 a year.

In the meantime I too little appreciated the many afternoons when my mother took me over the wooden railway footbridge from Woodstock Road into Finsbury Park. It happened sometimes that as we crossed the bridge a train would be heard approaching. It was impossible to see it from the bridge because the walls were too high (I revisited it recently, and although in the long interval my height has increased from two feet to six, they are still too high). If there was clearly no time to get across and see the train properly, I was allowed to kneel down and, as it roared under the bridge, to watch it through one of the wide cracks between the floorboards. I do not remember whether I was terrified or thrilled, or, if both, in what proportions. But it must have been this practice which established in me a horror of see-through flooring over railways and rivers, and of seaside piers with the water gleaming through; for one day the train whistle, when immediately underneath, let off a screech that frightened me nearly out of my wits. It also introduced me to the surprising knowledge (confirmed later in life when I came to inspect burgled houses) that fear can have the same effect as a variety of patent medicines upon which men have grown rich.

This episode, moreover, opened up to me the mercantile possibilities of false pretences; for the fright gave me a genuine attack of hiccups which nothing, it seemed, would stop. I find that every family has its own remedy for hiccups, but my mother's was that you must quickly eat something. She therefore faced the choice between taking me back home for a piece of bread or crossing the park to the refreshment room for something more interesting. The latter was quicker, and I got a penny sponge cake in a little paper bag. The ignoble sequel was that whenever I crossed that railway bridge thereafter, I appeared to be seized with hiccups, set off resolutely for the refreshment room, and had to be sharply called back.

Finsbury Park at that time differed strikingly from its present condition, in that there wasn't much grass. Indeed the big field adjoining the railway was totally bald, worn to the buff by the boots of Edwardian artisans as the local 'Speakers' Corner', at weekends entirely taken over by protest meetings. I remember once asking my father what all the meetings were protesting about and he said 'each other'. Today this field is grassed over, is equipped with goalposts, and accordingly harbours protest of a more universal, passionate, and informed nature. But the Finsbury Park of today is a part of the Parish of Hornsey, itself part of the Finsbury Division of the old Hundred of Ossulstone, County of Middlesex. Hornsey also embraces much of Highgate, Crouch End, Muswell Hill, and Stroud Green; and having once upon a time called itself Haringay, it has now become Haringey. It was in my much-loved Finsbury Park that the supporters of Thomas Woodstock, Duke of Gloucester, assembled to form a league against the favourites of Richard II. This, too, was the place where 'the citizens of London' had gathered to present petitions to Henry VIII, and even to Edward V (who reigned for 75 days in 1483 and was 12 when he was murdered with his brother in the Tower).

Finsbury Park, that is to say the open park itself, is a relic of the days when the London housewife had nowhere to dry a day's washing. There is an old ballad called *The Life and Death of the Two Ladies of Finsbury that gave Moorfields to the City for the Maidens of London to Dry their Clothes*. It has this verse:

> Where lovingly both man and wife
> May take the evening air
> And London dames to dry their clothes
> May hither still repair.

But when the 120 acres of Finsbury Park were provided in 1857 by the Metropolitan Board of Works (later the LCC, later still the GLC) as 'a recreation ground for jaded Londoners', the Board of Works was only giving back to Londoners what they had previously possessed in Finsbury Fields on the outskirts of a very much smaller London. One of the early Crusaders killed in the Holy Land was called Sir John Fines. His two daughters, after a period of mourning of 300 days, solemnly buried his heart (brought back from the Holy Land by a soldier) in a place to which they gave the name of Fines-Bury. In 1315 the manor was taken over by the City of London Corporation; and from then on the fields of Finsbury became the northern playground of London.

They are also memorable as the place where I first assisted in flying a box-kite, by sending paper messengers up the string to join the tethered monster as it darted to and fro in the sky. And I was introduced there, by a group of boys unknown to me, to the most recent and sophisticated of playtime gadgets, the flying propeller or 'whizzer'. At that time this was an immensely popular toy, largely no doubt because of the daring experiments then going on with 'heavier-than-air' flying machines—Blériot was to cross the Channel in a biplane in 1909. And without doubt it was a highly dangerous one. A metal two-bladed propeller, of about four inches span and having a rifled centre hole, fitted down over a 12-inch metal rod with a threaded screw. You forced it up and off, making it revolve madly, by means of a free-moving finger piece, and it span through the air like some toyshop anticipation of today's UFO. It cost sixpence-halfpenny in the shops, and accordingly had to be saved up for. I believe there were some bad accidents to faces and eyes; there was a brief experiment with rubber propellers, which proved hardly less dangerous than the tin ones; and the whole idea seems to have disappeared by about 1914. I have never heard or seen any reference to it since.

One afternoon I was returning across the footbridge from the park, this time with a neighbour who sometimes took me out with her own little brood—I think there were four or five children, though they may not all have been hers. She was a music teacher, and lived round the corner in Perth Road. It was at about the time of day when the infants' school in Wood-stock Road was emptying. And on that day I saw and heard (or anyway identified) my first piano-organ. Thus early did I learn, and begin pedantically to maintain, the little-known difference between it and a barrel-organ—which produces its music by means of a revolving barrel pitted with holes and slits. 'Coo look,' shouted one of the boys, much older than the rest of us, 'a barrel-organ.' She told us it was a piano-organ, and I suppose she made us understand in some way that it was a mechanical piano. It was the shape and almost the size of an upright piano, it was on two wheels, and it had barrow handles. By contrast a barrel-organ, she said, was small enough to be hung from the shoulders by a strap. They were both played by turning a handle, but the barrel-organ sounded like a wheezy little harmonium and the piano-organ like something between a cheap stentorian harpsichord and a boy running a stick along some railings. We all came to know this particular piano-organist that day, for we were allowed to stand and caper round him as he played. I don't doubt that he was hoping to collect pennies from the mothers fetching their children from the school, though I forget whether he got any. He was a wizened little man with no teeth and a perpetually shaking head; and he more often than not had a larger companion to pull the heavy piano-organ along. Once at least I saw a donkey between the handles; and indeed donkeys were an added attraction for the children and (probably) pennies.

The piano-organ was popular. There were even those who, living in quiet roads, loved to hear it from indoors. (My father was not among these.) Robert Whitelaw, E. V. Knox's classics master at Rugby—he was Rupert Brooke's godfather—actually hired two to play at intervals under his windows whenever he was correcting examination papers. But I don't doubt that it was a nuisance to many people who wanted and needed quiet. Indeed one day my elder brother, who hadn't been of the party which met the musician I have just described, was sent out by my mother to give him a penny and ask him to go away, my father being asleep at an unusual hour because of his police duties. Harold was missing on this errand for so long that Annie, our unpaid resident maid-of-all-work, was at last despatched to find him. She found him in the next street, proudly turning the handle of the 'organ'.

A much less exciting instrument was the hurdy-gurdy, a kind of portable harmonium held to the tummy and supported on a stick, usually played with a handle but sometimes with a keyboard like that of an accordion. Those with a handle of course played only pre-arranged tunes, but on those with keys the music had to be produced by someone with the necessary skill. Both kinds, it seemed to me as a child, always played hymn tunes, offering absolutely no invitation to the dance. By contrast the piano-organ, I was to find later, had an enormous repertory; and I have heard on it everything from the *Sailor's Hornpipe*, to which its staccato notes were exactly suitable, to Rossini's *Stabat Mater*, to which they were not. Notes lasting six or eight bars were sustained by rapid repetition—the boy with the stick and the railings. Men with piano-organs often played the latest 'pop' hits, sometimes with a man or woman to sing the song while someone else went round selling the sheet music.

If you were a man of good character you could hire a piano-organ for the day upon depositing ten shillings, usually from a huge repository wherein at night they stood in silent ranks; and all the money you collected was your own. If you were not a man of good character, as to which the proprietors were usually well informed, you could not hire a piano-organ for the price of rubies; and this, I have been told, led to a considerable amount of impersonation, proxy, and sub-letting.

Two other barrow-men regularly frequented the school precincts in the summer months, both selling ice cream but one of them offering also something called hokey-pokey. This was an inferior kind of ice cream, but it was distinguishable also by the fact that the men who sold it (always, for some reason, Italians) used to cry their wares, which the ice cream men of the time for some reason did not. 'Hokey-pokey, pokey O', they shouted, the final 'O' always coming out an octave higher than what had preceded it, so that from a distance the 'O' was all that you would hear. I have seen it suggested that when we all thought the Italian vendors were shouting 'hokey-pokey' they were really shouting 'O che poco', meaning 'Oh, how little!' I do not understand how anyone could suppose this to be true, but certainly it was a phrase that lent itself to rhythmical shouting, and those who had no penny for a lump of hokey-pokey (the great majority) would call after those who had, with the derisive envy of the have-nots:

> Hokey-pokey, penny a lump,
> The more you eat, the more you jump.

The barrows were brightly painted, usually white picked out with gold, and each carried two drum-shaped containers, one for 'real' ice cream and one for hokey-pokey or, sometimes, water-ice.

All these Italian ice-cream vendors were known as Jack, even though a high proportion of their barrows bore the legend 'Joe Assenheim's Ice Cream'. Many of them carried, in addition to the biscuit 'cornets' into which they slopped our helpings of ice cream with a wooden spoon, a row of tiny glasses, about the size of an eye-bath, in which you could sometimes get a 'taster'. As the children came rushing out of school, the barrow would be surrounded by a dozen of them shouting 'Give us a taster Jack!' And Jack sometimes did, no doubt choosing his moment strategically; for to keep a crowd's attention made him conspicuous, popular, and therefore successful. The taster was no doubt a justifiable 'loss leader'. I can't remember ever getting one.

Jack also played an unconscious but important part in my own instruction in family strategy. If my mother bought me one of his ice creams she always conveyed to me, I forget how, that my father would not approve and must on no account be told. What came through clearly was the awful threat that if he *did* get to know it would be the very last ice cream with which Jack would be allowed to supply me. I'm sure I didn't know at the time, but the reason was that my father regarded the Italian ice-cream men as dirty people, and their product as what he would professionally call 'not of the nature, substance and quality demanded'. This meant that they kept their mixing tubs under the bed. And I believe this clash of authority between my two admirable parents made a lasting and probably exaggerated impression on me, or at any rate that it was symptomatic of some larger disagreement that gradually became evident as I grew older. It has also left me with an irrational response to ice cream of any kind, quality, or price, and this has persisted throughout a long life: the feeling that ice cream must always be consumed furtively. There is something slightly unspeakable about ice cream, which is all the nicer for it.

As I recall the benign personality of Jack the ice-cream man, I realize that there was always to be seen sitting on his gaily painted barrow a little brown dog wearing a ruffle round its neck and a muzzle over its mouth, decorations which seemed mutually contradictory. I thought his name was Chip (it was probably Gyp). And the muzzle, I supposed, was to prevent Chip from licking at the ice cream, an arrangement which I considered clean but cruel. I was sorry for the little dog, with his caged-in face. Fairly soon I was to learn, since every dog you saw anywhere out of doors was muzzled, that muzzling was then the law of the land: rabies was an ever-present danger, and any dog not wearing a muzzle could be seized by the police (they kept huge rubber gauntlets for the job, and years later I was myself to use a pair, rather ineffectually and without enthusiasm). It's very seldom today that you see a muzzled dog; and when you do it is not because his bite is toxic but because the biting is slap-happy and not properly thought out.

*

I can clearly remember my first day at school, at the beginning of September 1904. I had waited for it long enough, watching for many months the playground scene from our first-floor window, and taking it to be a *tableau vivant* based on Casey's Court. Casey's Court was a comic-paper development from a 1902 music-hall sketch called Casey's Circus—in which, it is interesting to recall, Charlie Chaplin had appeared in burlesque: it included a crowd of street urchins playing at being grown-ups in a London back-alley, and it was these who were developed into a 'comic strip'. I thought they were wonderful, a mad little community wherein everyone did exactly as he liked, there was no authority (though there was a local policeman for laughing at), and happiness prevailed through the Rule of Unreason. One of the children's Christmas annuals of those years, I forget which one, always covered its spacious endpapers with a kind of Brueghel assembly of the Casey's Court inhabitants, grotesque pygmy figures with big heads and splay feet, all deeply absorbed in individual acts of mischief. I had pored over these pictures for hours, yearning for their fantasy-world in which you could use an enormous funnel for pouring treacle down the back of someone's dress, a see-saw as a means of reaching high-growing apples on neighbours' trees, or an ultra-long skipping-rope tied at one end to the handle of a piano-organ, so that the person turning the rope (from the other side of the road) also played the music, while a line of stunted Casey's Court inhabitants held hands and skipped.

That first day at school began with crushing disappointment, the Casey's Court image destroyed. First, I had long seen myself crossing the road to the INFANTS gate, rushing into the playground and becoming at once absorbed in whatever was going on. I was quite prepared to rush about aimlessly at first, picking up the real purpose of it as I went along. Instead I was *taken* across the road by my mother, people actually saw me being held by the hand; I was led firmly through the playing children (who hardly spared me a glance), and was conducted across a huge empty hall to a table standing next to a piano. And there, while my mother and a teacher talked about me several feet above my head, I watched a sobbing little girl whose legs were being sponged down by one of the teachers. When my mother had gone, her departure almost—and mercifully—unnoticed by me in the circumstances, I asked the teacher what the little girl was crying for. It was a little boy, she said, not a little girl; and he had had an accident. I was to find that among the smaller scholars there were several in this epicene state, their mothers' reluctance to 'breech' (or britch) them persisting even into their school days. But these were the boys who went to school at the age of two and half and, even so, could not yet be regarded as 'house-trained'. (Much of the house-training had to be done by the long-suffering teachers.) I was wearing serge shorts, which I remember because they tickled my legs— they were probably cut down from something or other; new black boots of which I was suffocatingly proud; and a woollen jersey which made me too hot. Breeching, by the way, had almost the status of a domestic crisis, with neighbours popping in to admire the emancipated victim and the new clothes in which he was being emancipated. I have seen a photograph of my cousin Herbert Speed which portrays him in girls' clothes at the age of four, and my brother Roland must have been at least three before he was dressed as a boy. It was to be many years before I learned that little boys at that time wore dresses not because their mothers were grieving that they hadn't turned out to be little girls but because no one had yet invented plastic or otherwise disposable nappies. In these unisex days everyone goes into napkins, plastic pants, whatever 'woollies' are needed in cold weather, and an all-in-garment called a Babygro. After that, it's dungarees all round.

The second disappointment of the day, a truly crushing one after those months of anticipation, was that when we got to half-past ten and playtime, a steady rain was falling and we had to play in the hall instead of out in the playground: a poor substitute and a betrayal. And yet because of it I learned two valuable lessons, each to last a lifetime. First, if your bootlace comes undone and trails on the floor it is advisable not merely to refrain from running but to walk with your feet very wide apart; otherwise you will step on the bootlace and come a cropper. The mechanics of this were explained to me by a teacher who untied her own shoelace and gave me a demonstration. Second, if it is your very first pair of lace-up boots you may get your first lesson in retying the bow from a young teacher who has never really learned to do it herself. It must have been such a teacher who showed me how to make two loops, place them side by side, and then tie them together in a knot. I tie my bows like that to this day.

It can't have been long before I was introduced to educational technology. It took the form of a wooden-framed slate on which one wrote, drew, or doodled with a squeaking slate-pencil, and which always seemed to bear oval yellow stains whereon you could make no mark at all. (I never found out what these were.) I have never understood why we had slates. They couldn't have been cheaper than paper and pencil, they were always getting broken, and they were in no sense a preparation for anything you would have to use when you had grown up. We also had little trays of sand, in which we wrote and drew with wooden skewers. Why, again? I remember the briefest of pleasure in these new things, soon to be drowned in the disappointment of not having paper, pens, and ink. But there were lessons at which everyone had an abacus—we called them counting frames and (it is said) I set off much infuriating merriment at home by calling them counterpanes. I think an abacus is the perfect instrument by which to discover, very early in life, that one is non-numerate; to find that one is, indeed, unable to relate sizes, quantities, and measurements to any conceivable arrangement of little beads on wires. I do not know why the abacus failed to inspire the counting part of my brain; but although I was soon able to comprehend that if you took four away from seven, the seven became three, and since I was totally indifferent about what happened either to the four or to the three, any grouping of beads on a counting frame left me cold.

So figures had a meaningless life of their own, and although many years later as an accountant's clerk I was always able to cast a long column of figures more quickly than most of my colleagues, I simply do not know why. Throughout my schooldays I never understood arithmetic or algebra, or why the compilers of our textbooks had their baths fitted with two taps which, by controlling the flow of water in *and* out at differing speeds, enabled their owners to lie in them and think up hideous problems. At one stage we were having thrice-weekly 'mental arithmetic' tests whose sole purpose, it seemed to me, was to uncover our stupidity in order to do nothing whatsoever about it. The teacher would read out ten questions from an assortment of printed cards he kept in a drawer, and we were supposed to put down the answers without doing any other writing or figuring, a restriction I never personally found limiting. I hadn't the slightest idea what these answers were, but owing to our cramped classroom conditions I was able to see what surrounding scholars thought they were, and thus to adopt and share their errors and successes. This must have gone on for a long time, for I found that the same questions cropped up repeatedly and I got to know the answers by heart. I suppose this must have satisfied the teachers that progress was being made.

And before I leave the classroom I must record that never once, in my twelve years of schooling in various parts of London, did I come across a teacher or a textbook able (or perhaps permitted) to convey the fascination and excitement of those twin subjects, history and geography. They were twin bores: heavy-hearted subjects, dull, stripped of nearly all the magic and the human interest to be discovered years later in 'adult education'. The history lessons were, it seemed, judged to be sufficiently human if they were larded with fancy legends like Alfred and the Cakes, Bruce and the Spider, Canute and the Tide, and Turnagain Whittington. Looking back, I have come to believe that History should tell a child the meaning of current events, the things going on around him, and *then* work backwards to the ancient world; while Geography should help him to understand how climate and birthplace affect the nature of man and the way his instinct for self-preservation will shape his own story. As he goes up through the school the child should run this course over and over again, each time with a fresh socio-political theme. What history I ever learned I was to get, in due course (a euphemism for middle age), from Gibbon, Froude, Macaulay, Wells, Toynbee and the marvellous teams of scholars who compiled the Oxford and Cambridge Modern Histories.

*

The playground was far more interesting than any of these interruptions (except reading). I was rather slow to learn that you were not expected to rush about simply because all the others were rushing about. They were rushing about with some kind of purpose, and the thing was to discover it and join in. In my case, this stage developed as a period of watching and

and weighing up; of realizing, in particular, that playground games were of two main kinds. First, those depending on some kind of permitted apparatus such as spinning tops, marbles, cigarette cards, conkers, paper darts, bats and balls. (For safety reasons some kinds of apparatus were not allowed in our playground at all, and these included hoops, roller-skates, scooters—the first I ever saw appeared in 1905 and was promptly impounded—bicycles, kites, and the 'whizzers' I have described on page 21.) Second, those demanding little apparatus or none at all, which included Tig (or 'he'), Poor Jinny, Hot Rice, Hi Jimmy Knacker, Fivestones, and Hopscotch. Each of them merits a brief description, since they were purely local versions of national games. From 1906 onwards the scooter was being condemned by grown-ups as vehemently as skateboards have been in recent years, and your hopes of possessing one depended on two qualities in your parents: first, having the money for such things, and secondly, not sharing the sombre view that they were dangerous, wore out one shoe before the other, and made you grow up lop-sided. All the scooters I remember from childhood were home-made from old bits of floorboard and pram-wheels; and I cannot remember the first of the shop-bought ones, though by the 1920s they were made of brightly painted boxwood and had rubber-tyred wheels.

The spinning tops were of two kinds, the 'throwdown' and the whipper. A throwdown was usually a pear-shaped wooden ball with a long metal peg at the small end, the wooden body being grooved to take the folds of string. You bound it up tightly with the cord, held it between forefinger and thumb with the left-over string bunched tightly in the remainder of your fingers; and as you threw it down from shoulder height you jerked the string to give the top an extra twist as its peg struck the ground. Until you were really expert its peg didn't strike the ground at all, and your twisting energy merely sent the top rolling ignominiously and swiftly away on its side, looking ridiculous. I didn't master it for years, and miserably envied any boy who could do it. But once the trick was known you could take part in a variety of competitive games, the most popular of which involved coaxing the spinning top with your middle finger on to the stretched palm of your hand, held close to the ground, and then tipping it on to its side among an arranged group of pebbles, little shells, or fivestones. It was then that the otherwise ignominious rolling about became important, for the object was to move as many stones as possible before the top became still. As for the whipping top, its control was always a bit of a mystery to me. Nevertheless it was so much easier than that of a throwdown as to be almost sissy for people over five, though you could condone it in girls of any age and even in mothers and aunts. For one thing, you started it spinning with your two hands, which anybody could do; or, more rarely and expertly, you bound it up with the string of your whip, balanced it on its peg, steadied it with the forefinger of the non-whipping hand, and then smartly pulled the string away, making it revolve fiercely.

The best whipping top was mushroom-shaped, because here the string, being wound round the stalk, had more coils to unfold and span the top more strongly. Once it was spinning you lashed it along the ground. There was absolutely no skill in this. At each blow the string coiled itself round the top, which tightened the coils by its own motion, and then as you pulled the whip away you gave fresh impetus to the spinning. Various skills developed as you ran into difficulties. If the spinning top ran off the footway into the road, you didn't need to stop it and pick it up again: there was a way of applying a double jerk to your whiplash that would make the top jump the kerb—I am speaking, of course, of a time when the roads were empty of traffic and the approach of any vehicle was announced by the distant clip-clop of hoofs.

Marbles seemed to be a game for the aristocrats among us, or the better-breeched. The only marble games we knew about (I believe there are hosts of others) required that each player should have a lot of marbles, and the leading marbles people carried their wealth, meggies and alleys (or 'taws') together, in a little cloth bag closed with a draw-string. Of them all I remember only 'Pyramids', a game in which one boy arranged all his marbles in a three-sided pyramid on the ground and drew a chalk circle round it. The rest of us then shot at it in turn with our own marbles, flicking each one by pinching it between the knuckle of the bent thumb and the curve of the forefinger. For each shot you paid one marble to the boy with the pyramid. But if you hit the pyramid (which very few people did) all the marbles which then rolled out of the chalk circle belonged to you; and then the pyramid had to be rebuilt for the next contender. Some pyramid boys amassed untold marble wealth through the over-confidence of the poor, the boys with no more than two or three marbles to their name. And we had among us 'marble barons', like the tobacco barons who control the secret economy of an English prison. Woodstock Road School at that time had a marbles economy which, so far as I know, was unique. The various means by which marbles were extracted by the strong from the weak included blackmail, intimidation, entertainments tax, and entrance fees to games of playground cricket and football. I remember paying a group of bigger boys two marbles to get out of the school lavatories and go home after school. But one of the respectable ways of getting marbles, which I was then too young to exploit, was the shoe-box peep-show. You could generally beg an empty cardboard shoe-box from a Stroud Green Road shop. One end of the box was then cut out, leaving a half-inch margin to which you could stick a square of tracing paper, butter-muslin, or something similar that would let in the light. You cut two eye-holes at the other end. And then with cut-out cardboard figures filched from old scrap-books (or you could laboriously make your own) you mounted some silhouetted and harrowing scene like the Execution of Lady Jane Grey. Boys would pay 'a meggie a peep' with the identical readiness that has induced generations of holiday-makers on seaside piers to put good money into slot-machines in the hope of finding out What the Butler Saw.

And then there were cigarette cards. Most of the games we played with cigarette cards could, I suppose, have been played with any bits of cardboard of the same shape and size; but the cigarette card was a popular 'flicking' missile among that majority of boys who lacked the tenacity of purpose to acquire complete sets and take care of them. (I collected only one complete set: it came from Player's Navy Cut cigarette packets and depicted all the current 'heavier-than-air flying machines', from the Henry Farman biplane onwards. I wish I had it now.) In the playground, and sometimes in the street, we drew a 12-inch circle on the ground about three inches away from the wall. You stood six feet away from that (in the street you simply stood on the kerbstone) and 'flicked' a card against the wall in the hope that it would drop into the circle. A card that did this earned its flicker five points. When all the cards had been flicked, you took it in turns to 'tip' into the ring, with your thumb-nail, all those left lying outside it, one point for each. When you failed your opponent took over. And when all the cards were in the ring the game ended.

At Woodstock Road School there was a resident caretaker who told us that the game of conkers was originally played, not with horse-chestnuts but with the shells of snails and winkles. (A conker is a little conch.) I once heard him telling a group of boys how you could make the string-hole in such a shell by using a red-hot meat-skewer held in a thick cloth. But we had an Uncle George in our family, a man with his own conker-tree, an acknowledged authority on the conker, who remembered that in the original game you had to press the apexes of the contesting snail-shells together between the palms of your hands, with your fingers interlocked—and go on pressing harder until one shell broke. Country boys used to make it a condition of the game, rigid but messy, that the original tenants should be in their shells at the time. The owner of the unbroken shell was the winner.

No one seems to know when chestnuts ousted shells, or indeed when they were first hung on strings instead of being crushed in the hands; but I've always supposed that boys would have been certain sooner or later to find a use for these shiny brown fruits, seductive but inedible, which lie on the ground in such profusion in the autumn. (I have a vast conker tree at the moment which, in a September gale, can sprinkle a whole lawn with conkers; and my daughter started it in a flower pot when she was very young.) My brother Harold as a boy had a conker which, at school, had smashed 36 others, a 'thirty-sixer'. He went to stay with our Uncle George and proudly took it with him. Uncle George scornfully produced one which, he said, was a 455-er, an unheard-of thing which should have aroused Harold's suspicions. When it had reached 466 at the expense of Harold's champion, Uncle George revealed that it was a stone from the beach at Folkestone, cunningly painted to look like a conker. We never ceased to regard this as an example of the treachery sometimes found in otherwise good men, and although our uncle laughingly made a gift of his false champion to Harold, it was accepted with a grimace and was never used again.

There was an out-of-season variant of the conkers game in which I never took any part. It transferred the endurance test from the conker to the bare knuckles, each boy taking turns to hit the other's closed fist with his own. I never saw any boy endure this for long, but I've heard that in sterner times the little idiots would bash all the skin off their knuckles rather than give in.

As I recall it, I am astonished that the relatively simple art of paper-modelling should have virtually disappeared from the lives of children for so long—from, I suppose, the First World War until the arrival from Japan of 'origami' a few years ago. At my first school I watched small boys and girls making model cottages, 'tidy boxes', steamships, table lamps, sentry-boxes, windmills, and above all paper darts with directional heads.

At one period there was an astonishing craze for folded paper darts, and fusillades of them in the playground at playtime. But these were gradually superseded by a kind of dart that would actually stick into a softwood surface and stay there; and this, I have always thought, was ingenious enough to have earned immortality for an inventor who remains, nevertheless, unknown. To make the sharp end you filched a 'Jay' nib from somebody's pen, and pressed the point down at an angle on a desk until the nib snapped across the middle. This, for some reason, left a pair of very sharp points like rigid little horns. You split a matchstick for about half an inch and pushed it over the blunt end of the nib; and then, having similarly split the other end of the match, you arranged therein two pieces of folded paper to make fins or 'flights'. (With use, of course, the match would gradually split right along and your dart came to pieces. You could prevent this by binding the middle with cotton or with stamp-edging, but it seemed scarcely worth while.) This little dart was almost as efficient as the pub dart of today, though it had a much shorter life—and if you made it carelessly it would revolve in the air as it flew. It also led to endless trouble with school authorities and with parents who, if they disliked chalked targets on their wooden doors, disliked even more the pockmarking of those doors with dart-holes.

But there were games which you could play even if you hadn't a possession in the world. I suppose that after the Woodstock Road period I would have scorned to take part in 'Poor Jinny is a-weeping', but at that time, round about 1905, I happily joined the girls in this ancient rune without (I believe) having any idea as to what it was all about. Our version of it ended with the words, which everyone duly put into action:

> Kiss her once, kiss her twice,
> Kiss her three times over.

And then I was very glad that I was never the Jinny in the middle, for I much disliked being kissed; but I don't think it dawned upon me that I was excluded from the role of Jinny because I was a boy.

I classify Hot Rice as a non-apparatus game, for although we usually played it with a rubber ball—and somebody therefore had to provide one—it could be played with a pebble, or a screwed-up ball of newspaper, or a small bundle of rags tied tightly round the middle. Any number of boys, but usually from four to a dozen, stood in a circle three or four feet apart and tossed the ball quickly from one to another round the ring. As soon as someone dropped it the boys ran off in different directions, and he had to catch them all in turn, helped in the process by the growing number of boys he caught, until the last but one was captive. The solitary boy then left was the winner. I thought it was a glorious game, no game ever devised has given me more ecstatic, sweaty and crimson-faced pleasure, more determination to hold on to a catch.

Less satisfying was a game called Hi Jimmy Knacker which, in our probably unusual version, produced some nasty injuries and (I remember) cost one boy all his front teeth. A boy would stand with his hands against a wall or, preferably, grasping some railings. He was bent so that his back was horizontal. A second boy jumped on and held tight. He was followed by others, who piled themselves upon him and upon each other until his legs gave way, whereupon there was much rolling on the ground and pointless shouting and laughing. In a more dangerous version, dispensing with any wall or railing, the first boy merely rested his hands on his knees: and it was this method which, as a rule, produced the injuries. It also produced unsuspected Samsons, boys who didn't necessarily look very strong but who, we found, could actually stagger about for a short time with three or four others on their backs.

Many other games which absorbed my contemporaries in playgrounds failed to absorb me. Hopscotch, for example, I merely watched, never understanding the rules—and always wondering why it was played only by girls. Certainly it began as a boys' game. After I had left school I found that it was very occasionally played by boys, but this seems to have been but a brief revival. 'Among the schoolboys in my memory,' wrote Joseph Strutt in 1801 (*Sports and Pastimes of the People of England*), 'there was a pastime called Hopscotch.' And it 'consisted in hopping on one foot and driving forward a flat stone, a fragment of a slate or tile, etc., from one compartment to another of an oblong figure traced out on the ground, so as always to hop over or clear each scotch or line.' But this wasn't the game I used to watch. In our version the 'scotch' or court was certainly a chalked rectangle on the ground, divided into ten numbered squares; but a girl would stand on one foot in square No. 1, place the stone in square No. 2, hop in and pick it up, hop back, throw or slide it into No. 3, hop there and pick it up again, and continue thus right round to No. 10—if she could—hopping all the time, and knowing that she was 'out' the moment she put the raised foot to the ground, for whatever reason. In 1886 *The American*, Vol. XII, remarked that 'the well-known boys' game of hop-scotch dates back to the beginning of the Christian era'. But the boys in my part of London were scorning it in my time. I wonder why? The girls were very good at it. Any male challenge to it might have been risky.

Fivestones similarly was for me a spectator sport; but in this instance, it seems, it had been taken over by boys from girls, for although I never saw girls at it I find, today, that all the historical references to fivestones accept it as a game for young women. You could buy a set of fivestones for a few pence and usually they were shaped to resemble the knucklebones of a sheep (which, apparently, is what they actually were when the game was invented). You could play it alone, of course, which was dull and boring; or you could compete with one or more opponents, which sustained much argument and artful sleight of hand. When I saw it played, a boy would arrange the five 'stones' on the back of his hand, throw them in the air, and try to catch them all in the same hand quickly turned over. In another version the stones were arranged in a circle on the ground, you threw a ball in the air, and before catching it in one hand you had to pick up one of the fivestones—which had to be taken in a certain order. I found this more popular when, at the age of nine, I got to Fulham in 1910; but in Finsbury Park you couldn't have called it a popular game.

It was while we lived in Woodstock Road that I became involved, by association, in my first experience (it was far from being my last) of what would now be called street vandalism. An older boy and girl had taken me, after morning school, to a sweet-shop—I remember that for some reason the grown-ups called these sweetstuff-shops—on the corner of Stroud Green Road and Woodstock Road. On the way back we passed a milkman's barrow, or what I later came to know as a milk perambulator, which stood unattended outside a house. In those days this was a deep three-wheeled barrow or truck, with a pram handle, a 50-gallon milk-churn in the middle, and oval lidded cans hanging all round its edges. At that moment there was no sign of the milkman. The boy with me, moved by I know not what daft impulse, danced up to it and pulled round the handle of the churn, intending I suppose to send a spurt of milk into the roadway. Then he couldn't turn it off, and as he struggled frantically like the Sorcerer's Apprentice he saw the milkman coming from, I suppose, about fifty yards away. The milk was now gushing all over the road and along the gutter at my feet, a sea of dazzling white. The boy and girl ran back into Stroud Green Road as fast as they could cover the ground, and I stood where I was, a shocked and (for once) innocent spectator. Having stopped the flow of milk, the angry milkman grabbed me roughly and asked me where I lived. Very frightened, I pointed across the road to No. 101. It was my gentle mother who opened the door, but my father happened also to be at home (I didn't understand in those days how fathers could sometimes be at home during other fathers' working hours) and he took command. I was told long afterwards that his interrogation of the angry milkman reduced the poor man to anxious agreement that I could have been no more than a helpless spectator. My father then wrote to his employer explaining what had happened. I have always been interested, remembering this episode, to reflect that it took place before the 1908 Children Act was in force; that therefore there were no Juvenile Courts; and that if the milkman had 'had the law' upon my two companions and myself for wilful damage, we should have had to go before a magistrate in the Police Court as if we were grown malefactors. You could be sent away, in those days, to a residential 'industrial school' at the age of five if your parents were unable, or unlikely, to stop you emptying other people's milk churns.

This would have been a miscarriage of justice. But justice, it turned out, was to go on mercifully miscarrying, and I was now approaching the age at which I was to be allowed to play in the street. We were moving house, and the street in which I was to play was called Corbyn Street and was about a mile away from Woodstock Road in a district, embracing no more than half a dozen streets, which was then rather more respectable. Today, I find, the difference is even more marked: last year I accosted a denizen of Corbyn Street and sought his opinion. 'Woodstock Road?' he said, aghast. 'I wouldn't live down there if I was a squatter.'

3

FINSBURY PARK 1906-1910

Our arrival at Corbyn Street in 1906 remains in the memory as a confusion of bare floor-boards, echoing rooms in which it was satisfactory to shout and whistle, and the smell of new paint (which I have always loved). But it is also memorable for the birth of a particular curiosity which has always gone unsatisfied: why, I continually asked my parents, did we now have to say *Corbyn* Street, accentuating the first word, whereas we had always said Woodstock *Road*, stressing the second? When you ask grown-ups this kind of thing, they usually sidestep it by denying the premiss; and you should never ask it anywhere near bedtime, which will be summarily and unfairly advanced. By the time I had convinced everyone that it was only *streets* which went unstressed, and that whereas we said *Oxford* Street, etc., we always said Stroud Green *Road*, Seven Sisters *Road*, Tollington *Park*, Crouch *Hill*, and so forth I had probably become a sickening nuisance. It was years later that my brother Harold, newly steeped in his school history of Ancient Britain, came up with the idea that originally every highway was a 'street' (OE straet), and that it was only when we began thinking up fancy names like Road, Park, Hill, Avenue, Gardens, Crescent, Close, Terrace, and Grove that we moved the accentuation to show that we knew we were departing from the norm. Meanwhile I accepted *Corbyn* Street, though neither then nor later did I find out who or what Corbyn was. I dare say he was the man who built the houses.

These were terrace houses, with six rooms including a kitchen but no bathroom. The lack of a bathroom seems odd because there were two lavatories, an indoor (upstairs) one and an outside one, the former being rather less spartan because its wood was varnished and its floor covered with linoleum (we called it oilcloth). In the latter the pan was boxed in with unstained and unpainted wood, and had a hinged wooden lid. In every Corbyn Street house whose intimate parts I saw this feature was identical. I came to believe that the wooden protection was a recognition of the fact that, in icy weather, people were always cracking the pans by standing on them to unfreeze the ball-valve in the cistern above. Before we moved in my father had the smallest bedroom—it was on the half-landing—converted into a bathroom, on the floor of which we had a shiny patterned linoleum which ceased to shine when the room was full of steam. And then you could write and draw all over the floor with a wet forefinger, forget to begin your bath, and be sternly recalled to duty by a parental rapping on the door. (The hot water had all been carried up from the kitchen in buckets and would not be replenished.)

In all the Corbyn Street houses, as I believe in similar houses throughout the country, the detail was nearly identical. There was a living-room-cum-kitchen, with a table arranged just far enough from the side-window to allow for two or three children to squeeze in and sit for a meal. There was a sink and, near it, a roller towel—always, in our house, of 'huckaback', a kind of linen with a rough surface on which you could never get your hands dry but which was cheap and almost everlasting. Near the sink was a wall-mirror with a lidded compartment beneath containing hair brushes and an assortment of combs—including a little black scurf-comb with tiny teeth whose real but un-discussed quarry was nits and head-lice. There was a kitchen range with an oven, a whitened hearthstone, and a hob on which a black kettle very quietly hissed for most of the day. On hooks at each side of this hung a kettle-holder, a button-hook, and a toasting-fork. In the late evening there was firewood ('bundle-wood', penny a bundle from the itinerant 'oil man' at the door on Fridays) standing in the grate and drying for fire-lighting in the morning.

There was a central gaslight protruding from the ceiling—*not* hanging, for its support was a rigid length of gas-piping; and it was immediately and conveniently over the table at which the family had its meals, wrote its letters, did its homework and its ironing, and pursued its winter hobbies. I remember that at this time we had not yet arrived at the 'inverted' gas mantle, a little cup of incandescent asbestos netting into which the gas jet was projected downwards, to make a brilliant glow. Gaslight was always a kindly and yet perfect lighting. We were still using the upright mantle, and I understood the word mantle because it fitted round the gas-jet like a long slender cape. I can't remember why it was that gas mantles ever had to be changed, but I think it must have been when we hit them with paper darts, cushions or tennis balls, which they were not constructed to resist. In the 1914–18 war, by the way, the official dimming of all the gaslighting was always our first intimation of approaching enemy bombers.

At about that time there were heard the first rumblings of the coming gas-versus-electricity war; we ourselves were not to have electric light in the home until 1916, and all my reading and writing, at school and at home, was done by gaslight. For years to come, accordingly, spent electric light bulbs were in great demand, both by boys who had air guns or catapults and by a few people like Miss Cissie Coney who made them into balloons for hanging up in drawing-rooms. (The balloon craze was still on—this was 1906. The annual Gordon Bennett balloon race always started from Paris, and in 1906 it was won by an American who covered 400 miles and came down in Yorkshire.)

The back parlour in those Corbyn Street houses, which was between the kitchen and the little-used front parlour, was often considered superfluous as a parlour of any kind, and used as an extra bedroom. (There were three small bedrooms upstairs but there were usually a lot of people to be got into them, including grannies, lonely aunts, and lodgers.) And a back parlour was, again, almost stereotyped in its decor and furnishing. There was usually a seven-piece suite, upholstered with plush or leatherette and stuffed with horsehair which, in due time, worked its way through the covering to rub prickly stalks against the unprotected legs of small girls and boys—and even indeed the protected ones of their elders. This suite usually comprised four dining chairs, two easies and a couch. Later we seem to have used the word couch indiscriminately for sofa and settee; but I now believe that a couch had a half back and head-end only, and was for reclining on, while a settee was a kind of very wide armchair for three or four people. They were all the same to us and yet represented, I understand, ascending stages of gentility, with settee at the top. For some years I was careful not to call anything in our house a settee.

My brother Harold, on the other hand, derided all such delicacy where there were legitimate grounds for oneupmanship. We differed from all our neighbours—though not, I believe, from a million similar households—in having a French brass mantelpiece clock which formed, unconvincingly I always thought, the centrepiece of a decorous flirtation involving two brass eighteenth-century peasants who spent all their time leaning on it. The whole affair was always covered by a big glass dome. Harold (or was it I?) told the neighbouring children that this clock was of solid gold, and there can be absolutely no doubt that this, totally untrue though we knew it to be, gave us a powerful ascendancy in the district. I'm not sure that I myself would have put it about, but once it was done I enjoyed the prestige happily. And when we moved to Fulham in 1910 we re-established it, to find its potency undiminished. Flanking the clock, at opposite ends of the mantelpiece, were two black metal casts (iron, I suppose) about twelve inches high, of rearing horses whose halters were being tugged by a naked man on foot. And these, with other less impressive bric-à-brac, all stood on a dark red plush-covered mantelshelf fringed with hanging bobbles.

All the soft chairs had embroidered or crocheted antimacassars on their backs, and an infernal nuisance they were. I thought for years that they were to prevent visitors acquiring head-lice from each other, as in first-class railway carriages. I understood nothing about Macassar oil and its seemingly unique properties as hair-grease for men. (I still don't. Why on earth should a kind of rather malodorous vegetable oil, from one tiny area in what we now call Indonesia, have covered the

soft-backed chairs of Europe, North America, and British India
with crochet-worked slips that were always falling off?)

At Corbyn Street our *front* parlour for some years contained
nothing, although the windows were decently curtained; and for
this there was the highly practical reason that there was nothing
to put in it. I think its furnishing began eventually with the
acquisition, in exchange for a vast collection of trading stamps,
of a jardinière, in which was placed a big flower-pot containing
—of course—an aspidistra. After that the curtains were slightly
parted in the daytime so that passers-by could just see that
we too had an aspidistra, but not the emptiness beyond. Some
of our neighbours had a 'false blind', a twelve-inch strip of lace-
edged and cream-coloured linen, tacked to the top of the
window frame, for show. A tasselled cord hung from the centre
of it, which you tugged at your peril—it didn't pull anything
up or down and you had better leave it alone.

*

A baffling recollection of that period is that nobody seemed
able to swim across the English Channel, though many people
already seemed to feel that it was there to be swum. Invariably
these were pictured in the newspapers as fierce-looking muscular
men with big black moustaches and their arms folded across
hairy chests as they faced the cameras. Today they contrast
strangely with the fragile-looking schoolgirls who are always
doing it with such apparent ease. (As I write this, an American
child has just gone across in a little over seven hours.) Holbein
was the name of one man who was always at it; and at school
some confusion arose from the fact that he also seemed to have
painted a portrait of Henry VIII, a reproduction of which hung
in our school hall. It made the king look a very square fat king,
and was believed to be the original of all the kings on the playing cards. All the swimmers gave up after about twenty miles,
and everyone was deeply impressed by the almost unimaginable
feat of swimming for twenty miles or for twenty hours, and by
the dawning realization that swimming the Channel had now for
some reason become impossible—as to which there were many

theories, about tides and currents, and undertow, and a deep-sea subsidence somewhere off Dover that had changed everything. This was because we all knew that a Captain Webb had done it in 1875—'without a life jacket'—and no one had done it since. One of the men always failing was a Mr T. W. Burgess, whom my father had met and in whom, accordingly, we all took a great pride and a proprietary interest, talking about him at school as though he were a personal friend. I think it was in 1908 that he again failed twice, although at one attempt he had swum more than fifty miles. I was beginning to fancy myself as a long-distance swimmer (I had recently done two lengths in the local swimming bath, an instructor walking along the side to shoo me away whenever I looked like grabbing the rail); and I felt very sorry for these men, especially Mr Burgess, spending much time poring over their press photographs. In our bedroom Harold and I had a large press photograph of Mr Burgess using a 'Sandow's Developer', a long, powerful spring terminating in two handles which you pulled apart (if you could) with your arms fully extended. Its inventor, Herr Eugen Sandow, was a German professional strong man and weight-lifter, a much-photographed man-mountain of rippling muscle who was currently used as a nickname for any undersized male weakling exposed to group humour. I forget whether Mr Burgess ever did get across or whether he resentfully gave up trying when other people began swimming across in large parties. In 1951 there were successful crossings by eighteen people in one day. How is it that the Channel swim, like the four-minute mile for runners, could ever become a commonplace instead of an impossibility?

There was much unemployment at this time—1906 to 1910; street begging was frequent and its practice took many forms designed to keep it within the law. The thing was, if a beggar appeared to be genuinely singing, or playing an instrument, or selling something in the street, he could claim, in answer to any charge of begging, that on the contrary he was offering value for money. And anyone wishing to refute such a claim on the part of a singing beggar was, *ipso facto*, setting himself up as some sort of a music critic. Reluctance on the part of policemen and others to assume this difficult role served as an encouragement to some of the most ghastly noises that have ever issued from the human larynx, and some of the strangest forms of instrumental music-making. A regular performer in Corbyn Street on Friday evenings was a legless man who sat in an invalid chair pushed very slowly along the middle of the road by his wife, playing *Yankee Doodle*, recognizably but unremittingly, on a one-string fiddle made from a cigar-box. This man started a craze for one-string fiddles, which the Corbyn Street boys constructed from every kind of box imaginable, usually wooden ones because they were easier to fit with a shaft. To achieve the necessary tension, you stretched a thin wire over the box and along the shaft by means of little staples, and then tapped small wooden wedges in until you thought you had found the right note. There was at least one boy whose repertory on this contraption extended far beyond *Yankee Doodle*.

Another tension instrument of great but inexplicable popularity was the jew's harp, a little lyre-shaped thing with a metal frame which you held against your partly-opened front teeth. It had a projecting metal tongue which you twanged with your thumb. I became excruciatingly proficient with the jew's harp, the kind that could be bought for twopence in toyshops; but mercifully it was very quiet always, and I found no way of increasing the volume of sound. The best local street performer with the jew's harp stood as a rule on the corner of Stroud Green Road and Seven Sisters Road, near the big gates of Finsbury Park; and for some reason, possibly to suggest that he was doing this kind of thing only until he could get work, he always wore a carpenter's bib and apron. His jew's harp was six times the size of ours and produced much more noise. It was the biggest I ever saw, and I never determined whether ours were toy replicas of such a thing, or his was a grotesque variation of ours. He was very good at it and had a regular audience of interested but penniless boys.

Street lavender-sellers were so numerous that it is sometimes now hard to believe that their trade has disappeared and that their lugubrious song will be heard no more. 'Won't yer buy,' they sang—

> Won't yer buy my sweet bloomin' lavender,
> Sixteen fine branches for one penny?
> Yer buy it once, yer buy it twice,
> It makes yer cloze
> Smell very nice.

The tune of it has always seemed to me exactly the kind of air that the great composers have liked to elaborate into symphonic or piano variations, but I don't know that anyone has done more with it than Noël Coward in his *London Pride*. Corbyn Street's most regular lavender songster was a swarthy woman in a man's cloth cap, a sacking apron, and an irregularly hung skirt which swept the ground behind her. She was always accompanied by three or four barefooted children. I have been surprised, by the way, to read in John Burnett's *History of the Cost of Living* that 'in large families it was not unknown for children to go barefoot *even at the end of the century*' (italics mine): it was commonplace as recently as 1910. Until about that time I always had barefoot schoolmates; and there was much competition among them for the discarded boots and shoes sometimes available for them in a big cupboard in the school hall. Odd to relate, the same cupboard housed (when it was not in use on somebody) the punishment cane with which, I suppose, a similar but sterner benevolence was given frequent expression.

The children accompanying street and kerbside traders were, as a matter of fact, a constant worry and grief to me. Why were they willing, or how had they been compelled, to follow such a dreary and miserable life? I simply could not help imagining myself in their place, condemned by an accident of birth to this doleful shuffling along suburban roads in the wake of a ululating and wretched parent, never (so far as I knew) having any fun or a moment to play and yet never running away. Why did they not run away? I grieved about them often and, in a futile sort of way, still do.

On Sunday afternoons there came, of course, the muffin man with his handbell and the huge tray of muffins and crumpets balanced so skilfully on his head, resting on what looked like a collection of cloth caps compressed by the weight of the tray into a suitable cushion. One of the questions with which I plagued my elders was why the muffins were always covered with a green baize cloth, and I never got any more satisfactory answer than that the muffin man's cloth had *always* been of green baize. My father (and therefore my mother) would never buy food from street sellers unless it was of the kind that could be washed—watercress, apples and so on. So I don't think we ever had street muffins. But we were fascinated by the muffin man's balancing skill, his brass handbell, and the slow rotation of the long tray as he turned round, usually opposite our house it seemed, to see whether anyone wanted him.

My mother would never think of buying from the man who strode the centre of Corbyn Street howling 'WIRE ABBESS' but actually selling wild rabbits. These, said my parents—and, come to think of it, all the grown-ups—produced dark meat and were less appetizing than the Ostend rabbits you could buy in the shops. Why *Ostend* rabbits? I never did understand why a great Belgian seaport should produce the only desirable rabbit. (I am now reliably told that these were also known as Flemish Giants, and were indeed reared in Belgium as tame rabbits for the table; sometimes weighing as much as 15 or 16 pounds. There must have been a considerable import trade in them.) Nor can I understand why rabbit has disappeared from our dinner tables, on which it made a brief reappearance during Hitler's war as if we classed it with horse or dog meat, to be eaten only in adversity.

Daily there was a cat's-meat man, and ours always came pushing a home-made box-cart on an old pram chassis. He was followed by a retinue of expectant cats, who knew it to be full of feline kebabs—small bits of cooked horsemeat pushed on to wooden skewers, a halfpenny a skewerful. If, at the house of a regular customer, the cat's-meat man got no answer to his knock or ring, he pushed the kebab through the letter-box and collected the halfpenny the next time round. Most cats would polish off the meat as soon as it came through the letter-box, and the homecoming cat-owner would find on the doormat a clean-licked skewer. There were rival cat's-meat men who, instead of putting their delivery through the letter-box, would wedge it under the street-door knocker. Such men underestimated the agility of neighbouring and uninvited cats, who were actually seen to dislodge such prizes, after perhaps several failures, and feloniously make off with them. At one time this development was being seriously discussed as an ingenious and safer method of 'knocking down ginger', demanding only an old piece of fish, the nerve to go and lodge it under someone's door-knocker, and a hungry cat to be held firmly until the right moment had come.

The law about begging at that time recognized the ingenuity of those beggars who hoped, often with breathtaking impertinence, to be regarded as offering 'value for money'. For instance, in its protective attitude to beggars' children it prohibited their involvement, 'whether or not there is any pretence [sic] of singing, playing, performing, offering anything for sale, or otherwise'. I've already mentioned the 'pretence of singing' and the aesthetic judgements which the phrase imports, but a 'pretence of offering anything for sale' could sometimes be even more subtle, as when a man would shuffle down the middle of the road holding out a solitary box of matches. It is perhaps significant that my brother Harold and I, who had watched such a man go along Corbyn Street uttering some totally unintelligible cry, had much difficulty afterwards in getting anyone to believe we had seen such a thing. One box of matches? It was really going too far. But in busy thoroughfares like the Seven Sisters Road and Stroud Green Road it was certainly not unusual to see a man sitting against a wall, holding out one box of matches and obviously having no others from which to replace it if someone had the hardihood to buy it instead of merely giving him money. It was surprising, too, how often such a man sat with one leg stretched out and the trouser leg pulled up to reveal that the limb was artificial.

Safety matches then still cost only three-halfpence for a dozen boxes, despite all that Annie Besant had done, forty years earlier, on behalf of the hungry Bryant and May match-girls.

This sort of thing was of course the product of hopeless poverty plus the universal fear of what we then called 'the Workhouse'. From the nearest workhouse to us, which I think was in Hornsey Rise, there came regular reminders of all this in the form of single-file processions of 'female inmates' on their way to or from their 'daily walk' in Finsbury Park, dressed always in black coats and skirts, black straw hats, and black buttoned boots. Not only my mother but also my Grandma Hewitt, who was often with us, said that these poor women wore neither underclothes nor stockings, because 'the Parish' thought they were unnecessary for such people; and I think I can say that this information had the effect, when I was aged six or seven, of injecting into the pity and puzzlement my very first stab of prurience. It seemed to me at the time, though my recollection may well be faulty, that the 'male inmates' from the workhouse never walked in single-file groups but in twos and threes; and they wore grey jacket suits, black cloth caps, and an ordinary shirt with no collar or tie. I can't remember seeing children from the workhouse at all, though Charlie Chaplin related in his *Autobiography* that when he was a boy in the Hanwell workhouse, which was a few years earlier, the children did go for 'workhouse walks', a hundred of them two abreast, all wearing the 'hated uniform' and cruelly known in the neighbourhood as 'the boys from the booby hatch'.

I was not otherwise much aware of the poverty that must have surrounded me. Among my street playmates there was no one without shoes or socks, and among those at school there were none whom I could have named. But there were several whose mothers made them 'new socks for old', by cutting off the worn-out foot, sewing up the leg at the bottom, and then sewing a length from another discarded sock on to the top. The result must have been a frightful bootful of sock, but I don't remember that any of the wearers complained. I have never, in fact, ceased to marvel at what children will put up with in the way of makeshift, uncomfortable, inadequate or over-hot clothing.

Other memorable evidence of working-class conditions at that time was provided by the parents of a friend of mine living round the corner in Evershot Road. I never knew the parents and forget their surnames; I knew only Eric and Hilda, their son and daughter, who were twins—though they seemed to me less alike than even ordinary brothers and sisters. Eric told me one Saturday morning that his father, a railwayman, was in trouble because he had joined what I suspect was a kind of local commune, whose purpose it was to dig up and cultivate a piece of land adjoining Finsbury Park and belonging to the Railway. The participants, I believe, were mostly unemployed and desperate for food. I know now that in 1906 and 1907 this was being done in many parts of the country, the pioneers being a party of starving unemployed men who took over, without permission, a gravel field belonging to the local authority at Plaistow. Some of the landowners allowed it. Others took ejection proceedings against the men. I suppose that among the public at large there was insufficient sense of crisis: in both world wars a man who was willing to 'Dig for Victory' could usually get an allotment for nothing—and even the railway embankments looked like little hillside vineyards of vegetables.

The father of Eric and Hilda had been supposed by the railway authorities to be the ringleader in the Finsbury Park enterprise, and he was sacked. The story must have filled our household with vicarious worry, for I heard my parents talking about it repeatedly. I wish I knew the sequel, and how the man contrived to maintain his family, but it seems likely that Eric and Hilda disappeared from my life at that time because of it. What disappeared with them was Eric's large coloured football, which we took a long time to replace. (He always had to go home earlier than most of us, and he would—wisely—take his ball with him, whatever the state of play.)

It was at about this time, around 1908, that I learned about Florence Nightingale, the Crimean War, and 'The Noble Six Hundred'. There were special lessons at school about Miss

Nightingale, the Lady with the Lamp, and I think it must have been because she was about to be presented with the Freedom of the City of London: rare if not unprecedented in the case of a woman, and an occasion which would involve my father in the kind of extra police duties which meant disruption of the normal routines at home. At all events, there was a great vogue among the girls, both at school and in the street after school, for home-made nurses' caps, improvised white aprons bearing the Red Cross on the breast, and a demand for boys to lie down on the ground and be wounded soldiers. Someone spread the disturbing intelligence that Florence Nightingale had never worn the Red Cross on her aprons or anywhere else, because in the Crimean War the Red Cross hadn't yet been invented. The rumour was ignored (though I suppose it was all too true). In our own household the Lady with the Lamp suffered a partial eclipse when my father irreverently reported that she had failed to turn up to receive her Freedom of the City because (he said) she spent all her time in bed and wouldn't get up. At the last minute she had sent a substitute. I think we all felt that the entire fuss had come to nothing. I suppose Miss Nightingale may have been spoiled by the fact that, only the year before, the King had conferred upon her the much-coveted Order of Merit (which most people seem to think she got from Queen Victoria).

Miss Nightingale had also been the subject of prayers and special lessons at a Sunday School attended, none too willingly, by Harold and myself at the New Court Congregational Church in Tollington Park. This is a huge church which you enter through lofty Corinthian columns, and in those days I thought of it as the very Temple of God. Our attendance, however, must have been too spasmodic to qualify us for the annual Sunday School Treat, for which several hundred enviable Sunday scholars would set off with packed lunches in horse-drawn brakes from the corner of Seven Sisters Road for some wistfully un-known destination 'in the country'. I truly longed to be among them. On the Saturday mornings of their departure I never failed to see them off, many of my friends among them, hoping, perhaps, that I might by some happy chance get the ride which I hadn't earned. Each brake carried a man with a cornet or bugle, whose function (and whose generally unmusical stridency) seemed to have no more significance than that of adding to the general din and excitement.

In 1960 the Tollington Park Congregational Church, by the way, having been without a minister for two years, became St. Mellitus's Roman Catholic Church (Mellitus being the third Archbishop of Canterbury, sent thither from Rome in 601). It is an interesting thought that if it had been an Anglican instead of a Reformed Church edifice, the Diocesan Redundant Churches Committee would probably have allowed it to fall down or become a Bingo hall rather than let the 'traditional' Catholics have it.

To return to Miss Nightingale, it happened at that time that I was able to speak with authority among my street companions on the subject of nurses and hospitals, for some months earlier I had gained immense local prestige by having diphtheria and then scarlet fever in quick succession. This had entailed a period of ten weeks in a hospital at Muswell Hill. I think I was about five and a half when I was put to bed one glorious summer afternoon at about three o'clock, and went without protest; an indisputable sign that I was too unwell to care much what was going on—but not too unwell to take note of subsequent events. I remember the clip-clop of the pony which brought Dr Noad's smart little gig, a brown pony with what I called 'white ankles'. Dr Noad always wore a brown bowler hat pitched well forward on his head, had bunched-up grey hair that stuck out at the back, and carried in his left hand a whip which he never seemed to use. Other boys' doctors seemed not to have gigs. They came on a bicycle or walked, and I never discovered how it was, in those days before a National Health Service, that we were able to afford a doctor with a gig when there seemed to be so many ordinary things we could not afford. I never learned how much we paid him; but I knew that other boys' parents paid their cycling doctors three shillings and sixpence a visit (including medicines). Moreover those doctors must have done their own dispensing, for they employed boys on bicycles to bring your medicine to your door. Perhaps in those days, before we had drugs for everything, the greater part of 'general practice' was all bedside manner, squeaky boots, and bottles of coloured water.

At my bedside Dr Noad produced what was no doubt a hypodermic syringe, and told me that if I didn't make a fuss when he used it on me I should have a syringe of my own when I got better. (This lightheartedly vicarious promise, fulfilled by my reluctant father ten weeks later as I was on my way home from hospital, equipped me for three hectic days with a long brass garden syringe. On the fourth day it had to be taken from me because I was loosening neighbourly bonds by using all the local cats as targets.)

I must have been lucky, for diphtheria at that time was killing children by the thousand, and even among those who survived there were many who were sadly crippled. Mr Frank Swinnerton, for example, tells in his autobiography how his childhood bout of diphtheria left him paralysed for two years— 'one arm and one leg completely out of action, mouth twisted, speech inarticulate, had to be pushed everywhere in an abominable contrivance called a go-cart' (which had 'bamboo shafts and plaited seats fore and aft' and therefore must have been quite unlike the go-carts known to me).

I was taken to the fever hospital by hansom cab, my father's anxiety being so intense that he couldn't wait for an ambulance. (I have no idea what ambulance promptitude was like in those days, but there was a marvellous City service of City Police electric ambulances, and my father may well have judged all other ambulances by it, so much to their detriment that he wouldn't even try them.) My mother told me once that the good Dr Noad paid for the hansom cab himself. I heard long afterwards that there was a great row about this hansom cab trip, since it was a punishable offence to carry anyone suffering from a notifiable infectious disease in a Hackney carriage available for public use; and although the cabby may not have known he was carrying a diphtheria patient, whatever he thought when told to drive to 'the Fever Hospital', my father certainly knew and so did Dr Noad. It was my first-ever ride in a hansom cab, but sad to say I was in no mood to enjoy it. There were in fact special ambulances for 'fever patients', and we always regarded them with pity and horror, as if their occupants were victims of the Black Death. The children at Finsbury Park—and nowhere else that I can remember—would grasp their coat collars on seeing an ambulance of any kind and call out something like 'Grab your collar, Don't swaller, Never catch the Fever', or 'There goes the fever-van, Never touch the mealy-man'—the meaning of which I never did discover. There was also a superstition that, having seen an ambulance in the street, you must hold your breath and pinch your nose until you saw a black or brown dog. I never understood that either, and would never do it. My father told me that even the paddle-steamers on the River Thames were used as 'isolation boats' for taking fever patients to hospital.

It was during this long hospital sojourn, also, that I got my very first clockwork toy. It was a little tin traction engine, green and red; it was the cause of another row, and this time I did know about it. On visiting days we 'fever' patients had to stand about ten feet from the big closed hospital gates, our visitors standing outside and contenting themselves, if they could, with peering at us through the bars. The first time this happened I had the immense gratification of seeing my elder brother Harold in tears because he was not allowed to come closer to me. I remember watching him with gratitude and wondering why I wasn't in tears too on account of not being allowed closer contact with him.

On the day of the traction engine my parents had also brought me some eggs and apples; and my father proceeded to send these under the gate and along the path to me, one by one, lodged in the cab of the traction engine. This process took up the whole of the visiting period, involving much communal handling and winding-up of the traction engine, by visitor and fever patient alike. Not until it was time to go did one of the nurses see what had been going on, and then there was a great fuss about this unusual breach of the quarantine regulations. But there was nothing to be done, and the fuss had to be its own justification and sanction.

While I was in hospital I heard much gossip about the various sources, previously thought innocuous, from which you could now 'catch the fever': privet leaves; putting an iron key in your mouth; passing a smelly drain without a handkerchief to clap over your mouth and nose—even my father used to say sharply, 'Hold your breath and breathe through your nose', and Harold and I never dared to ask him how you could do both at the same time; sitting on damp grass—this led to something called rheumatic fever; eating wild mushrooms; wasp and bee stings; and trading with the 'rag, iron or bone' man.

Of these there were in the Corbyn Street area in 1906–1910 a considerable number of busy rivals, but they all used the same street cry: 'Rag iron or boner?' The extra syllable on bone was common to the vernacular, especially at the line-endings of popular songs and street versions of hymns. Elsewhere you might well have heard 'Rag bottle or boner', 'Any old ironer' and so on. But our men always offered to buy rags, by which they rather hurtfully seemed to mean discarded or even well-worn trousers, overcoats, and bedspreads; old iron, which always seemed to mean bedsteads, spring mattresses, mangles, and discarded kitchen ranges; or bones, and why would they want bones? I never actually saw them get any bones. I've been told since that they sold them to bone crushers, who supplied the farming world with fertilizers. Nor, in districts where they sought bottles, did I see them buy any bottles, or understand why they should want them.

Prominent among the 'rag iron or boners' was a man whose little cart always carried a number of tiny goldfish-bowls, the water in which had always slopped about until the poor goldfish, one to a bowl, were almost confined to the bottom. These were gifts for any children who could persuade their parents to come out with old clothes for sale or barter—the usual exchange at that stage being a china vase or flower bowl. Some thirty years later the goldfish business was stopped by law: the

Public Health Act of 1936 prohibits any 'rag dealer' from selling or giving food or drink to anyone, and selling or giving anything whatsoever to a child under 14. And in 1961 Parliament made it clear that this applied to the giving of animals, fish, birds, or 'other living things'. Had our legislators awakened to the fact that it is, after all these centuries of innocence, possible to be cruel to fish? They had not. The new law was concerned solely to prevent the spread of infectious diseases by the sale and collection of old rags; and a long-established system of barter by which an old pair of father's trousers equalled one nearly-dead goldfish came to an end because of the trousers, not because of the goldfish.

There was one other street spectacle which, after moving from Corbyn Street to Fulham, I was never to see again. This was the horse-drawn water cart; or, when I come to think of it, any kind of water cart. Corbyn Street was watered in hot dry weather from a large four-wheeled tank-waggon drawn very slowly by a nodding horse. It had a long sprinkler-bar at the back, which threw up the water in a wide and pretty fountain; and in this peripatetic shower-bath on very hot days it was not uncommon to see naked children dancing and shrieking happily. The driver never seemed to mind. Nor, in some instances at least, did the mothers: you would sometimes see a mother walking indulgently by the side of the cart and carrying dry clothes and a towel.

If, as I suppose, the water cart was called into existence by the unhappy effect of the motor vehicle upon dusty roads, it probably had a relatively short life. The metalling of roads, that is to say the use of broken stone for macadamizing, had actually begun in the 1820s; and it must be one of the very few benefactions hastened by the internal combustion engine. I can't remember what our street was made of, but although it was certainly a dusty street and liberally manured by horse traffic, it couldn't have been a mere dirt road by 1908. However, it was far from smooth, and if you fell down on it while running it tore your hands and knees open. It tore out the knees of my Norfolk breeches so often that in the end my mother sewed on large leather patches, of which I was deeply ashamed, trying to conceal them at school by letting out my braces so that I could tuck the patches down inside the tops of my turn-over stockings. But they never stayed put.

It was at Corbyn Street that we acquired a 'high pram' for my infant brother Roland, the first such vehicle to have entered the family. Harold and I were greatly interested in it, never having ridden in such a thing ourselves and now, alas, being too big ever to do so. One terrible day, when the pram was placed in the small front garden so that Roland could go to sleep in the sun, we unintentionally took the brake off and it ran out across the pavement, pitched over as it left the curb, and threw Roland into the middle of the road. We found him sitting up and examining the eight red 'stars' which had appeared where his fingers joined the palms of his hands, and which were now beginning to ooze blood. He remembers the episode himself (he was about eighteen months old at the time) but not the row which followed it.

However, the spray from the water cart certainly contained some carbolic, and the hot-weather sprinkling may thus have been merely an example of the current official anxiety about smells and 'germs'. And whatever the surface of the roadway in Corbyn Street, it was always possible at that time to bang cricket stumps into it; and the same was true, a year or two later, of Gowan Avenue in Fulham. It says much for the infrequency and the slowness of the traffic along those London suburban roads, in the years before the 1914 war, that you could play cricket on the crown of the road with sufficient confidence to warrant the banging-in of stumps. It was also a way of avoiding the endless arguments about the proper height of a wicket chalked on a lamp-post; but it had the disadvantage that, once a stump had been knocked out, it left a jagged hole in which it could not be put up again and the whole wicket had to be moved.

It was about this time, 1908 or 1909, that three epoch-making events took their place in my happily humdrum story. The first was the discovery, perhaps a little early, of the word *adultery*.

My father constantly used the word 'adults' where anyone else's father would have said grown-ups. And at about that time, as a man always watching his pronunciations, he shifted the accent from the second to the first syllable, where it rightly belonged. One morning I spelled out from the *Daily Graphic*, which he used to bring home from the City, the headline LLOYD GEORGE DENIES ADULTERY. I knew Lloyd George was someone of importance (he was in fact Chancellor of the Exchequer). His conduct was therefore inconceivable. To deny adultery, was, I supposed, to deny being grown up. It called for explanation, and my father side-stepped it as 'something I wouldn't understand'. It was dear Cousin Florrie who, in his absence one day, told me that adultery had nothing to do with being an adult, it was to do with husbands or wives being much too friendly with other people. (Lloyd George had in fact won a libel action against *The People*, which had called him an adulterer. I wonder if it had spoken too early?)

The second event was the birth of *The Magnet*, and the beginning of a great struggle between my brother Harold (now aged 11) and my father for its recognition in the household as suitable reading. Harold was one of that multitude of lucky and discriminating readers who, surreptitiously or otherwise, read *The Magnet* from the day of its birth. In due course the miraculous 'Frank Richards', who wrote the *Magnet* stories on Monday, became Martin Clifford to write *The Gem* on Wednesday, and changed again into Owen Conquest for writing the *Penny Popular* on Friday, won even my father's approval. The stories reminded him, he unexpectedly told us (for we never actually caught him reading them), of a far better series in his own youth called *Jack Harkaway's Schooldays*. Martin Clifford once fell from grace when Harold, hugging himself with glee over a copy of *The Gem*, innocently sought to share with my father his enjoyment of what he thought was a hilarious episode in the week's events at St. Jim's. One lot of boys, bent on extracting secret information from another lot, ambushed them in a wood near the school, tied them up, took off their shoes and socks, and began scratching the soles of their feet with pen nibs, to make them talk. And 'yells of fiendish laughter rent the glade', the author had written (the phrase lived in our family for years). It was not funny, my father thought. It was torture disguised as schoolboy fun, and it could lead boys to accept cruelty and torture as justified if they thought their motives were good. He was ahead of his time, I suppose, in this anxiety about the literary debauching of the young; but I cannot recall that either Harold or I ever scratched the soles of a captive's foot with pen nibs.

I do not believe that any writer has ever given me greater pleasure than this incredibly many-sided man Frank Richards. I can't remember reading him at that time, but within two more years I was hooked, and read *Magnets* and *Gems* until I had reached an age which I do not consider it necessary to reveal. I have always held it against Compton Mackenzie that he should have allowed himself, in *My Life and Times, Octave One*, to use such a phrase as 'wretched papers like the *Magnet*'. But in the same book he proclaims, rather than confesses, that he preferred *The Cock House at Felsgarth* to *The Fifth Form at St. Dominics*, a position from which he simply cannot be heard to pass judgement upon Greyfriars and St. Jim's. Nor could I agree with the unhappy George Orwell when, in 1939, he wrote his famous essay in *Horizon* on 'Boys' Weeklies'. The *Magnet* and *Gem*, he said, were 'vilely printed'. They weren't. He should have lived to see our newspapers today. Billy Bunter, he decided, was 'the one really first class character' in the *Magnet* stories, the one who will survive. Well, if he survives, it will be because of the resilience he displays when, in one unforgettable story, he short-sightedly dives into the school swimming bath when it's empty—and merely gets concussion. Or it will be because he is grossly fat, greedy, cadging, contemptible, a butt for everybody—and a fabulously impossible ventriloquist. He was a cause of misery to countless overweight children, but he is an impossible creation, a clumsy vehicle for contempt and ridicule, not 'a first class character'. Incidentally Orwell wrote that 'a series lasting 30 years could hardly be the work of the same person every week'. But it was, and his real name was Charles Hamilton; and there is absolutely no reason why it should not be one man's work given that the writer is neither well-paid nor lazy.

The third event was the arrival of the game called Diabolo, which quickly became a national craze. And I think this is the point at which to explain, for the need will now become increasingly clear, that from an early age—probably five or six in my case—our lives were dominated by my father's inordinate love of dictionaries. However intolerant he may have seemed about our chosen reading, and perhaps as an aspect of that intolerance, he lived by the dictionary and brought us up to do the same. No chair was, in his view, placed for comfort unless it had an English dictionary within arm's reach, and at the smallest hint of linguistic or semantic doubt or difficulty, he reached. In me, it remains an inherited characteristic; and here it directs me firmly to the dictionary's definition of Diabolo. 'The game consists', says the *Oxford English Dictionary*, 'in balancing and spinning a double-headed top on a string (which is supported on two sticks), throwing it into the air and catching it again.' Rather than a double-headed top, it might perhaps be described as having the shape of a straight-sided hourglass. The *OED* also says that it is 'the game of the-devil-on-two-sticks revived under the name of Diabolo'; and adds that its modern inventor 'was M Gustave Phillipart, a French engineer well known in the automobile world'. But it seems to have been much older than anyone in the automobile world, as M Phillipart discovered when he rashly sued William Whiteley Ltd of Bayswater for infringing his 'Diabolo' trademark. The Chancery Division of the High Court dismissed his claim on the ground that the word couldn't be registered as a trademark. It applied, said the Judge, to a popular toy known in England in the early nineteenth century as The-Devil-on-two-Sticks, and revived on the Continent in 1907. Strangely, although the game has long disappeared, many people seem to know the name of it, including those who can never have seen it played. At the time I am speaking of, you could see it being played everywhere, and in the neighbourhoods where it could be afforded the flying diabolo top joined the tennis ball and the shuttlecock as another object always needing to be reclaimed from the garden next door.

In less affluent districts boys were producing home-made sets. Certain brands of salt and some kinds of spices were sold in cone-shaped cardboard containers, and you could join two of these at their apexes by pushing a wire skewer right through them both and turning it over or burring it at the end. It never seemed to me very effective, but this may have been because I could never do it anyway, and I thought the shop-made ones ineffective too. Seldom, in any event, did you see anyone catch a diabolo top on the waiting string more than once and never, therefore, did I want a set of my own. This was as well, for I was never offered one.

At this period the boys' outfitters' shops, Isaac Walton, John Baker, Man and Boy, etc., sold little suits which, among those whose parents could afford them, amounted to a uniform and probably represented the last dying kick from the days when all children were got up as diminutive adults. A tweed or serge Norfolk jacket buttoning right up to the throat, surmounted by a huge white Eton collar (celluloid for week-days, starched linen for Sundays). There were always a few boys, and I was one, whose Eton collar was fastened with a press-stud bow, and I remember that among the rough-and-tumble of school horse-play this would pop out and fall on the ground a dozen times a day. (I saw this happen once to a black bow-tie worn by a dinner-suited and eloquent alderman, excitedly opposing me about something or other at a Students' Union meeting at Durham University. It won him what I thought a cruelly pro-longed round of applause, almost eclipsing the appointed theme of the debate.) Other boys' collars were merely fastened with a stud, sometimes with a kind of piston which pushed into a cylinder, sometimes with a hinged top that you could twist to a holding position once it was through the shirt and collar button-holes. Underneath all this in the winter was a very long flannel vest which bunched up in your breeches; and when this was new (my mother always made them) it had to be worn for a fortnight before it was washed because 'the oil in it was good for the skin' and would all be lost after the first wash; what kind of oil, and what sort of good, I never discovered.

The boys who didn't have Norfolk jackets usually had coloured blouses, plus jerseys in the winter. Such boys, generally speaking, wore shorts, as distinct from the button-up knee breeches that went with the Norfolk jacket. I consider it an unaccountable lapse of memory that this Norfolk jacket rig-out is the first regular outfit that I can remember, though I am quite certain that I didn't go thus to school at the age of three. There must have been a moment of evolution, from whatever-it-was to Norfolk jacket, which would be at least as momentous as the change from clip-on bow to hand-done necktie; and the latter I remember still with excitement, probably because of the inordinate length of time spent on my instruction in it by Harold and my father at different exasperated sessions. To this day I cannot do up a necktie in the mornings and think of something else at the same time.

Equal in splendour, no doubt, to the change from ready-made bow to hand-wrought tie was that from knee-breeches to long trousers or 'long 'uns'. At the time I am writing of, this was still many years away.

On our legs we wore thick grey woollen stockings with coloured turn-down tops. Even if you wore garters, these wouldn't stay up for long, and my father disapproved of garters as 'bad for the circulation'. If there was one habit among the boys of that period which was as common as the toss of the head with which girls then (and both sexes today) got their hair out of their eyes, it was the sudden stopping, in the midst of whatever kind of game or hurry, to pull up their socks from round their ankles. Our footwear was extremely varied. It varied, that is to say, from those who had none at all to those who wore smart lace-up boots from shops like Randalls, Mansfields, or Freeman Hardy & Willis. In between were boys who wore plimsolls (America had not yet taught us to call them sneakers) in all kinds of weather, and some who wore their brothers' (or fathers') handed-down and blacked-over football or cricket boots with the studs removed from the soles. No one, by the way, would have had the effrontery to wear brown boots. They were the mark of the Edwardian dandy, they went with loud tweeds and shooting jackets. My father once proposed to send the twelve-year-old Harold to school in a pair of his own hardly-worn brown boots; and the resulting row, before they were decently blacked over, shook the household and kept it shaking slightly for weeks. Harold would as soon have lain down and died.

Inexplicably to me, I was never allowed to go equipped with blakeys, small metal shapes hammered into the boot-sole so that the wearer was walking on metal. Only the poorer boys had them. They represented yet another class division, or perhaps sub-division, of which the unique peculiarity was that those with blakeys were usually ashamed of them, while those without felt permanently deprived. Blakeys had two attractions: on frosty days they gave the wearer an ascendancy over all others on the slides in the playground, and on any kind of day he could kick up showers of sparks from stone pavements like a newly-shod horse. I never had blakeys.

I suppose I could have bought them, with saved-up pocket money. I got a penny a week and was passing rich on it—I know people of my age whose weekly pocket money at that time was a farthing. Could you buy *anything* with a farthing? You could indeed, if you shopped around. There were many kinds of sweets to be had at four ounces a penny: 'ju-jubes' pre-eminently, though these I think were simply sugar-coated jelly shapes and not the lozenges of gum-arabic that the modern dictionaries declare them to be. For a farthing you could buy a foot-long strip (one inch wide) of breakable toffee called hanky-panky; or a sherbet dab—a triangular stick of black liquorice poking out of a paper screw of sherbet; or an Ally Sloper's lunch, which was a tiny 'plate of meat and two veg', all made of sugar (Ally Sloper was a comic-strip character); or a toffee-apple; or an ounce of tigernuts—and these now seem to me the oddest confection of them all. I disliked tigernuts very much, both the texture and the almost-sweet tastelessness, but bought and chewed them on Saturdays because a farthing bought more of them than of anything else. In some shops, and occasionally from ice-cream barrows, you could get a farthing drink of sarsaparilla, a bright pink potion made by boiling the dried roots of American *smilax* and alleged to be a tonic, with a number of medicinal properties which the modern world seems able to do without.

What you could buy for a penny was of course far more impressive than all these farthingsworths; and additional pennies were sometimes to be acquired by selling jam-jars to green-grocers (who used them for bottling fruit) and old newspapers to butchers and fishmongers. I was never permitted, as were some enviable boys, to use the family pram for this purpose; I borrowed a soap-box on wheels from an obliging neighbour and stacked it with as many jam-jars or newspapers as it would carry. I remember with some bitterness that more than once I had to bring the whole load home again because the market had been saturated before I got going.

With a whole penny to spend, as distinct from a Saturday penny to be spread over a whole week, you could go into Marks and Spencers' Penny Bazaar and pass an agonizing hour of ecstasy, patrolling the display counters with the penny in your hand. These were the ancestors of the modern super-markets, hypermarkets, jumbomarkets; nothing cost more than a penny, and a high proportion of the counter-space was allotted to toys, dolls, pencils, crayons, drawing and painting books, and sweets. The variety of little tin model vehicles available at a penny seems to me now, as I recall it, simply astounding. Admittedly they were not fitted with clockwork, you had to push them along or run them down slopes, but they were excellent little models (made, mostly, in Germany) of the motor vehicles then beginning to appear on our roads; and they included, I remember, a 'Vanguard' motor bus and a perfect model of the City of London Police electric ambulances.

And speaking of the penny, there is one function of that now forgotten coin which has always seemed to represent social injustice and sex discrimination at its worst; and that is the

system by which, in a world of public health authorities dominated if not actually monopolized by men, women and girls
have always been made to part with a penny before they could
gain access to a loo. Boys, I remember, needed a penny when
they wanted a cubicle to themselves, with a locked door. Otherwise they peed with the blessing of the proprietors, or, as it
were, on the house. Why, I always asked myself, should this
be? The penny impost survived countless changes in the mone-
tary value of the coin, it is true. But I first became aware of
the problem when, in Finsbury Park one Saturday afternoon,
I rejoined my mother outside our segregated havens just as an
exasperated woman was saying to her little girl: 'There—now
you *will* 'ave to walk 'ome!' My mother explained and my
puzzlement began.

In 1909 my mother died, after four years of intermittent but
worsening pain with cancer. For a long time I had seen her
only in bed or in a blue dressing-gown, and it horrifies me now
to recall the matter-of-fact way in which I accepted the pathos
of the situation. She was just someone ill in the house, always
ill. I try now to comfort myself (always a great self-comforter)
with the possibility that an exceptional memory has in this one
instance failed me, and that it all meant more to me than I am
now suggesting and recalling. It seems to me specially interesting, in writing what I intend and conceive to be an accurate
recollection of temporal things in my own childhood, that my
brother Roland's memory of our mother at this time is far
clearer than mine; and he was not much more than three years
old when she died. She is a vivid picture in my infancy, at
Woodstock Road, when she was taking me for walks and sometimes singing to me at bed-time; and then she fades until one
bewildering evening when I was called in, hot and sweaty, from
playing in the street.

I had been round the corner at the foot of Crouch Hill, where
in those days the horse buses coming out of Stroud Green Road
were halted so that a third horse could be attached for the
Crouch Hill climb. A willing boy who hung about there looking
available might sometimes be called upon to assist in the process

of harnessing, and his reward could be a free ride up the hill on top of the bus. (He had to walk back.) It happened to me only once, and then not because of any help I had given but because the boy who *did* help was seen by his Mum just in time and hurried off home. I had sat near the driver, who had a pro- jecting seat at the front and would sometimes converse with passengers over his shoulder. His whip stood in a socket ready to his right hand, and I was told that one day a woman had snatched it out and thrown it into the road because she was 'against all ill treatment of animals'.

I was beckoned by my father into the kitchen, where I saw my elder brother Harold (he was twelve) looking white and shaky. No doubt Roland was already in bed. Father spoke to Harold. 'What's the matter sonny?' he said. (He knew what was the matter, but it was always thus that he felt his way in diffi- cult situations.) Harold's whispered answer was, 'I think Mother has died'. I forget how it was that he knew. Half-sitting on the kitchen table, Father without another word put his arms round our necks and pulled us to him; whereupon Harold gasped and began to cry, while I stood puzzled but unshaken, wondering what kind of role it would be best to play. I was deeply ashamed that, by comparison with the elder brother whom I so much admired and tried to copy in every way, I could feel sufficiently detached to wonder how Father was actually feeling and what he would do next. The guilt has never left me.

I remember the welcome simplicity of the funeral. In those days even the comparatively poor spent incredible sums of money on 'a decent burial', some of them saving all their working lives in order to do so. But the domestic burial fund, where it existed, was regularly depleted in most families by the frequent deaths of the children: an infant burial at that time, on the simplest scale, could cost from £6 to £10. An adult funeral, if there were to be carriages and plumes and hired mourners and flowers, plus some kind of necessary meal for relatives who had come long distances, could cost £50. I had always dreaded any such pomp in our own family life. But since my mother was to be buried at Fulham Cemetery, where all her forebears were laid, there would be a long and expensive carriage journey. Accordingly the number of grave-side mourners had to be kept down to two carriage-loads, including the immediate family; and the whole thing, to my infinite relief, was kept very simple. It was in fact sufficiently unobtrusive to be almost (and of course reprehensibly) enjoyable; for the experience of actually riding in a four-wheeled 'growler' was something to be savoured, an adventure to be made the most of afterwards. Incidentally I remember my father admitting to Harold that he didn't know why it was called a growler; and it seems that to this day (to judge from the guessing in the dictionaries) neither does anyone else.

During my mother's last few months we boys had been looked after by my Aunt Carrie from Fulham, who knew, I suppose, what a handful she was taking on: Harold was twelve, I was nine, and Roland was four. I didn't realize it then but her own husband, my Uncle Frank, was seriously ill in hospital and thought not likely to live. In fact he died a few months later, and in due course there was a marriage (very much of 'convenience', I suppose) between my father and Aunt Carrie, one of the very first marriages permitted by the Deceased Wife's Sister Marriage Act of 1909. But by that time we had moved to Fulham, where my father had found a house so similar to the Corbyn Street one that it might have been transplanted there for us.

It was No. 50, Gowan Avenue, Fulham Palace Road.

4

FULHAM FROM 1910

And yet our new home had one supreme architectural difference from any building we had inhabited before: it had a balcony over the front door, supported on two imposing columns. So did every house in the street, so far as I remember, but no matter. We were proud of our balcony, and on the very day we moved into the house, while every room was in a state of chaos, I put a chair out on it and sat for a few minutes with folded arms; though probably not, I suppose, for more than a few minutes. There was soon to be a family schism over the pronunciation of balcony, Harold having discovered somewhere that it was the Italian word *balcone* and therefore pronounced bal-*coney*. Harold was full of these new ideas, and they were now being nourished, it seemed to me, at his new school, the Latymer Foundation Upper School at Hammersmith. He had been there for a term when we moved from Finsbury Park in August 1910. He had passed his 'Cambridge Local' examination, secured a place at Latymer, and spent the summer term staying with relatives in Hounslow. When he rejoined the family he brought with him two freshly acquired accomplishments. One was the ability to turn cartwheels in rapid succession, to be contrasted with doing only one and then falling over (I was never able, or anyway willing, to do any at all). The other was the ability to yodel, which he exploited with ear-splitting and non-stop skill about the house until he discovered that it had been purely fortuitous and bestowed upon him by the fact that his voice was breaking (he was then nearly fourteen).

Incidentally, he finally gave in over this bal-coney business when he came home from school declaiming a verse from something of Dryden's that he had encountered in English lessons:

> The maids to the door and the balconies ran
> And said Lackaday! he's a proper young man.

I have always remembered that the first thing my father did on getting possession of the house was to remove the folding doors that separated the front and back parlours. He took them off their hinges and put them down in the coal cellar. I'm sure his object was not to amalgamate the two rooms permanently, because the place of the folding doors was soon taken by heavy green velvet curtains, which were always thereafter in place as a partition. (They were opened at Christmas when we had a fire in each room.) But the folding doors were hideously painted red and yellow, and it had been done in the brief interval since my father first saw the house. He just wasn't having them. The importance of the episode is that it got him off to a bad start with our new landlord, Mr Hamm, who at that time lived next door. Mr Hamm, whom I remember as a tall slinking figure with thick spectacles and a straggling grey beard, duly expostulated that he had just had those doors 'gaily painted' and that it had involved him in considerable expense. And the thought of that expense is specially poignant if you consider the following advertisement in the *West London Observer* for 18 August in that very year, 1910:

Six-roomed houses redecorated, thoroughly done, twenty shillings. Ceilings from two shillings. Walker, 35 Godolphin Road, auxiliary postman.

And here are some housing rents and values as they appear in comparable advertisements in the same newspaper:

Furnished flat, sitting room, two bedrooms, separate kitchen, piano [*sic*], plate and linen. One guinea weekly. 5 Brooklyn Road, Shepherds Bush.

Room, furnished, suit married couple, everything for use, five shillings per week. 11 Crisp Road, Hammersmith.

Six-roomed house £195, 75-year lease, near trams; bargain; only wants seeing.

Indeed houses with 99-year leases and the offer of the freehold were commonly selling at £200. A year or two later there appeared this advertisement in the same paper:

Why pay rent when you can buy one of the splendidly appointed houses on the Crabtree Estate in the Fulham Palace Road? Each contains pretty entrance hall, two sitting rooms, three bedrooms, bathroom and scullery. Roofs boarded and tiled, bathroom tiled, electric light fittings supplied throughout, blinds fitted to all front windows. 99 years lease. Ground rent £6. Freehold can be had. Price—£300, of which only £35 need be paid down.

Yet my parents and their intimates, I remember, thought these were totally impossible prices, putting house-ownership far beyond the reach of such as they. The Crabtree Estate, it was said, was 'all too fancy', with its built-in electric light fixtures and its fitted blinds. The electric lighting in particular was all very well, but it 'impaired one's eyesight': I remember the phrase so well, for it set me wondering what other kind of sight there was. The Crabtree Estate must, we thought, have been getting a huge subvention from the electric-lighting companies, upstarts who were bent on doing us all out of our beloved gaslight at all costs. Our landlord never succumbed: we never had electric light until we lived in the City.

I don't know what was the 'average' artisan's wage at that time, and I have always doubted official versions, but in my mother's cookery book, dated 1910, the recipes are all based on a family income of thirty shillings a week—of which one quarter was reserved for rent. I know that the rent we paid to Mr Hamm was sixteen shillings a week, and that he got it every Friday morning with the regularity of sunrise. There were one or two houses in Gowan Avenue which had hot-water systems of some kind, but we had none. Nor was there any gas-burner in any bedroom or the bathroom. In the winter, going to bed and getting up were done in the dark, washing and bathing were done by candlelight. A bucket of hot water was carried upstairs on bath-nights, and the dilution of that with cold tap-water in the bath was a matter of sober foresight and judgement. I can't remember that any of this was regarded as in any conceivable sense a hardship.

Mr Hamm's disapproval over the disappearance of his painted doors may have been tempered by the fact that, a few days before our arrival, the drainage had been condemned by the local authority, the floors had been taken up in both front and back parlours, and the ground floor of our new abode accordingly comprised two gaping holes and two mounds of earth and rubble. Thus they remained for several weeks. Where the downstairs furniture was during that time I do not remember; but I clearly recall that, whatever may have been our parents' state of mind, a ground floor consisting of two craters seemed to my brothers and me a perfectly acceptable part of the excitement of 'moving'.

Of the three of us, only Roland had actually witnessed the emptying of the Corbyn Street house and the departure of the removals van, which Father had satisfyingly called a pantechnicon. (Why was this, we wanted to know? But, well-informed as he always seemed to be, he couldn't tell us, and it was no moment for consulting any of his numerous dictionaries.) Only Roland had stayed at Corbyn Street during the transition period after our mother's death on 9 August 1910. Harold was at Hounslow. And I, for the period of the school summer holidays, had been for part of the time billeted on our Grandma Speed in Munster Road, and for part of it on our Aunt Carrie at 51 Niton Street, Fulham Palace Road.

Grandma Speed, parent of the mother we had just lost and of our Aunt Carrie, occupied a position in our family comparable to the world stature of Mother Teresa and the Venerable Bede. We understood her, indeed, to be a saint. She looked like one. At this time she was over eighty: she lived to be ninety-six. She always had snow-white hair, her face was round, benign, rosy and smiling, her lips and hands always trembling; and it seemed to us that when she was not praying she was reading to herself from a huge illustrated Bible, for which purpose she always sat at a table. I was sometimes allowed, indeed I think probably encouraged, to browse in this Bible; and the one thing I remember from it is a little drawing, in the 19th chapter of Genesis, of what looked like a man with a sheet over his head. Actually this was Lot's wife as a pillar of salt, and there was a caption saying that modern expeditions to the Cities of the Plain in the Dead Sea area had found numerous little obelisks of sodium or potassium chloride, the inference being that one of them might be Mrs Lot.

Grandma Speed, who was a widow (I never knew either of my grandfathers) lived with her aged and unmarried sister Mary Ann (Aunt Polly to us) on the top floor over a shop at 213 Munster Road. It was a stationer's shop and its proprietor was her son, my perpetually ailing and delicate Uncle Alfred. He was my youngest Speed uncle, and of them all I believe the hardest-working. I have certain vivid recollections of that little shop, and eminent among them is the display of rows and rows of W. T. Stead's 'Books for the Bairns', little penny paperback versions of the old children's classics from *The Labours of Hercules* and *The Fables of Aesop the Slave* to *Grimm's Fairy Tales* and *The Stories of Hans Andersen.* On holidays and after school hours I used to stand behind the counter reading these, treating the little books with such care as would preserve their newness and saleability, and ready to call out 'Shop' if a customer came in for a writing pad, a packet of paper doyleys, some shelf paper, a pencil with a rubber on the end, or something that my Uncle Alfred had been laboriously printing, in the other half of the shop behind a partition, on his pedal-operated printing machine. Specially significant is the memory that if a child happened to come in unaccompanied he was instantly regarded with suspicion. Children didn't have money to spend in such shops, the customers were nearly all grown-ups, and even the Books for the Bairns were bought by the old for the young, as 'improving' books they probably wouldn't have bought with their own rare pennies.

Munster Road, Fulham, was, I am convinced, an excessively ugly thoroughfare, and yet there hangs about its remembered ugliness a charm and (for me) a happiness beyond explanation. Not far along the road from No. 213 was a long brick building bearing a huge enamelled blue-and-white advertisement panel which said BATEY AND SONS FOR MINERAL WATERS.

These very large sheet-iron hoardings were, no doubt, symptomatic of the commercial confidence and slow change of that period, as was the habit of picking out advertising slogans by inserting coloured bricks in the entire end wall of a corner building. But it is a curious and puzzling memory that, for me, the regular pattern of a high brick wall, or of the totally blank side of a large building, was comforting, virile, and in a way fascinating. Perversely, I saw a kind of beauty in its ugliness and spent much time idly contemplating the endlessly repetitive side-end-side-end-side of the brickwork. At the back of my mind, I suppose, was the thought that every single brick had been trimmed and placed in position by skilled hands; perhaps even a dim realization that no machine would ever supersede the bricklayer. I have no doubt, though, that it was during this childish and happy contemplation of brick walls and the angularity of buildings that I stumbled upon an aesthetic truth that has entertained and puzzled me ever since, giving me the illusion of original discovery: namely that there is no such thing in the whole of Nature as a straight line. If, I told myself, man had never made his appearance on the earth, the only shapes and contours everywhere on it would be curves, circles, ellipses, parabolas, and spheres. Therefore in any painting or drawing the juxtaposition of straight lines and 'natural' background, for example even the railings round the park, was like a statement of history and experience—and unfailingly interesting even where it was not pleasing. Window frames, as the foreground of a picture, have always delighted me; and I understand why it is that they should have attracted legions of artists.

I must have stayed many times with Grandma Speed; and the fact that I was tolerated there at all suggests to me today that I may not have been so boorishly ill-behaved as I seem to remember being—or perhaps that she was a stronger disciplinary influence than my memory allows. The truth is that she radiated, without effort, an almost frightening goodness that seemed to identify her as a person with one foot naturally inside the Gates of Heaven. Harold, Roland, and I, when we thought about her, thought in whispers. But I loved staying with her; and the bedroom I shared with her fostered son, Jim Elderkin (who was about ten years older than I), had a window from which, for hours after I was supposed to be in bed, I could look down on a busy scene of shopping and hurrying and gossiping in Munster Road which could have been the inspiration for all the drawings of George Belcher. There has always been, for me, a special London magic about Saturday nights, even about the phrase itself, and the scene from that high window every Saturday night was endlessly interesting. The spirit of the thing was epitomized, a few years later, by Barry Pain of the *Evening News*, in a book which he actually called *Saturday Nights*.

Exactly opposite was a greengrocer's shop, the outside of which was brilliantly lit by a row of naphtha flares. Soon after midnight there was always a last-minute crowd of women seeking reduced-price vegetables for the Sunday dinner. Many of these women had come straight from the butcher's where they had just bought, also at a last-minute price reduction, the so-called 'Sunday joint'; and this was all too often no joint of any kind but scrag end of neck or even a collection of offal. Some of them had certainly been in the local pubs for several hours, emerging only at closing time—which in those days was 12.30 all the week but 12 midnight on Saturdays. And among those who *could* buy joints there were many who, when they went to church or chapel on the Sunday, handed them in at the local bakery to be roasted during Divine Service. The worshippers collected them in a warmed enamel dish on the way home. This custom, I was told, began when bakers were not allowed to bake bread on Sundays, and made good the imposed deficiency in their earnings by baking other people's meat instead. I suppose some sort of Sabbatarian principle was thus preserved.

Jim was seldom home before midnight. He was a vigorous, simple, rather gauche teenager who was to play (all unconsciously, I now suppose) a formative part in my life for the next five years, and then to drop out of it completely. I am ashamed of not knowing where he came from or why it was that Grandma Speed had fostered him (she had eight children of her own), but we were not encouraged to enquire. We all liked him and we 'took him as he was'. My father, I learned years later, was uneasy about our occupying the same bedroom but no doubt found it difficult if not impossible to explain his objection. He need never have worried, as a matter of fact. There will be more about Jim Elderkin. His relevance at the moment is that he nearly always, round about midnight, brought me home something unsuitable to eat, biscuits or monkey-nuts or sweets, and thus kept me wide awake through many hours of anticipation. Those waiting hours I spent in my flannel night-gown at the high-up window of No. 213, looking tirelessly down at the evening kaleidoscope of Munster Road, Fulham.

It was thus that I got to know about drunkenness. When I first saw men and women reeling about, or fighting—the horrify-ing spectacle of women slogging at each other was really quite common—or standing on the kerb waving their arms and shout-ing, I thought at first that they were idiots. At Finsbury Park my brothers and I had grown accustomed to the presence of idiots in the streets, and without in the least understanding it, had accepted that there were strange grown-ups who publicly behaved in much the same zany fashion as we did when we wanted to make each other laugh. We were told that they were ill and 'couldn't help it'; and the thought that they were simply ill, and might (but for the grace of God etc.) have been members of our own family, was enough to exclude us from any of the mockery and amusement indulged in by some of our street playmates. I think it was a long time before it fully dawned upon me that drunkenness is in fact a kind of tem-porary and self-inflicted idiocy, but the Munster Road spectacle was the beginning of understanding. I remember seeing women trying to injure each other with drawn hatpins, and at least one woman trundled off to the police station—or somewhere—in a conveniently available builder's barrow. None of this was ever funny to me: it was only horrifying and infinitely sad. And to this day I hold that to laugh at a 'comic drunk', even fictionally presented, is no better than laughing at a cripple.

Harold, I remember, later found drunkenness funny, and Roland still found it puzzling; I found it frightening. I very much doubt that either of them has ever been drunk in his life, and I am quite certain that I haven't. We were all brought up to abhor Strong Drink (my mother always used the actual phrase) and to regard pubs as places of sin. The anti-pub theme was so dominant at home that all my life I have felt uneasy in pubs, subconsciously expecting at any moment to be recognized therein and publicly denounced as a traitor; while the whiff from a pub, if I pass its open door, almost makes me quicken my stride. I still do not relish the synthetic bonhomie of the man with his elbow on the bar counter, nor am I cheered by the loud laugh that fades so quickly the moment he feels himself to be unobserved. I am uneasy in pubs.

*

Fulham in those days seemed an interesting place with a group personality and a sense of history; whereas, when I walked around in it on a recent visit of rediscovery, it seemed to be little more than a geographical expression. The estate agents, in particular, are now prone to call it West Chelsea. But it is 'a parish in the Kensington Division of the Hundred of Ossulstone in the County of Middlesex', according to Samuel Lewis's *Topographical Dictionary of England in 1881*, and 'consists of several irregularly built streets, some of which are paved, and lighted with gas. . . . It is a place of considerable antiquity, the Danes having fixed their headquarters here during their invasion of England in 879.' And 'the manor house, or Palace of Fulham, has been from a very early period the usual summer residence of the Bishops of London.'

Once while I was staying at Niton Street, and I think it must have been during the Whitsun holiday of 1909, there was a Great Church Pageant which convulsed the district in a way that not even a Cup Final could do today. The Bishop of London, Dr Winnington Ingram (he later became Archbishop of Canterbury), had offered the use of his Fulham Palace grounds for the occasion. I have before me the sixpenny Pageant Handbook, sumptuously produced on the proceeds of advertisements, calling for volunteers to take part in the Pageant. Aspirants had to fill in a form saying 'I am willing to take part in every performance or find a substitute, to take the part allotted to me by the Committee, to wear the costume for the part, and to reimburse the Committee for the outlay incurred in providing my costume provided it does not exceed . . . ' And they had to indicate whether they wanted speaking or non-speaking parts, mounted or singing parts. Jim Elderkin had applied for a part in the Pageant, and to the boundless indignation of us all he was turned down. We never got to know why, unless it was that he couldn't sing or ride a horse and that he had a rather shuffling walk which turned both his feet out. Harold said he might have been quite good at non-speaking.

But I remember that the children of Fulham, of whom I contrived to be one though I was not yet at school there, were given a huge garden party in the Bishop's Palace Grounds, and sent home with white cardboard boxes containing a bun, an orange, and a commemorative medal. 'In pageantry reverently produced,' said the handbook, 'we see a vehicle of enormous power educating through the eye and the mind the people of this country in the history of their Church.'

Luckily for the children of Fulham, the Church had given a large part of the Palace grounds to the Borough for use as a public park. In 1886 the Church Commissioners made over to the District Board of Works a long riverside area then known as the Tide Meadow, part of the Bishop of London's manorial property. The London County Council gave £5,000 towards building an embankment, and in 1899 it was extended by the acquisition of Fielder's Meadow. Our Gowan Avenue landlord Mr Hamm had some small financial interest in a strange project, the brainchild of one of his tenants, concerning the almond trees in Bishop's Park. This man, discovering that the almonds were fit to be preserved and sold, made the Borough Council an offer for them. He got about three hundredweight of almonds for £10 and sold them at an enormous profit. I found that we were expected to regard this operation as in some way discreditable, and I could never understand why. It imported into the austere life of Mr Hamm a touch of comfort.

The Bishop's Park was the playground of my next five years. It was also the place where I acquired the jaundiced view that park-keepers were skilfully trained killjoys, going around in brown serge uniforms and brown bowlers looking for me and my companions to see what they could stop us doing. I have been told that their job was, *inter alia*, to see that the children in the Park enjoyed themselves, but in this they must have felt misunderstood. The fiercest of them, whom for some reason we called Solomon, always carried a hazel switch; and this, no doubt quite unlawfully, he used upon our legs or behinds as a form of instruction he seemed to think superior to his own rather simple though vivid vocabulary. Looking back, I don't doubt that whatever he was supposed to be doing to our lives, we made his life a misery.

It was on the Bishop's Park pond and paddling pool, which had an imported sandy beach, that my first and only model yacht *The Sunbeam* outstripped all others. If it beached and was stranded on the little central island, it could be rescued only by taking your breeches off and wading across with your shirt gripped firmly round the middle; and all the yachtsmen knew that it was the part of wisdom to take the breeches under your arm and not leave them to the mercy of passing predators on the mainland. The Bishop's Park riverside embankment stretched the full half-mile along the Thames from Putney Bridge to Fulham Football Ground; and it was during the summer of 1910 that this was the scene of an exciting encounter between the formidable Solomon and my own father.

Harold, Roland, and I had all somehow acquired little wooden lifeboats, each brightly painted blue and white and about twelve inches long. They had neither sails nor engines, and they had to be either pushed along or pulled with a string. My father, realizing that this was rather juvenile, had the bright idea of using them as drogues, that is to say attaching a long line to the gunwale of the boat about one-third of the way along from the bows, dropping it carefully from the Park embankment and pulling it against the tide. With 100 yards of strong twine you could make a lifeboat work its way almost 100 yards towards mid-Thames. But it became obvious after a little practice that, to get the boats clear of the embankment wall and to avoid the tangle of driftwood always slopping about there, we needed long canes or rods. So we got 6-foot bamboo canes and tied our boat strings to the ends of those. We were very conspicuous doing this from the embankment railings and, I dare say, were doing something that had not been seen before. Solomon appeared one day and shouted angrily to us that fishing from the embankment was not allowed and we were to clear out. We weren't fishing, we said. We pointed to our little boats and nervously watched Solomon's stick. He glared at the boats, hesitated no more than a moment, and ordained that they were to be hauled in and taken away. Then my father revealed himself as, however improbably, of the party. (So *this* was Solomon, he seemed to be saying to himself.)

He asked to be shown the Parks regulation which forbade the floating of toy boats on strings from the embankment wall. Solomon glared at him, in no sense taken aback, and wanted to know what it had got to do with him. You will understand our father's domestic prestige if I say that we all waited breathlessly for the heavens to fall. Nothing came down. When my father declared himself as patron and leader of the toy-boating party, Solomon told him the Parks Regulations were to be read on a notice board at each of the Park gates. And, said my father (no doubt chancing his arm), they had nothing to say about toy boats on the river. If they supported Solomon's strictures, then the boats would be pulled up. If not, Solomon had better go away. It was at this moment in a drama we were watching with trembling enjoyment that I set up a sudden howl because my boat had broken its string and was careering madly down river on a strong ebb-tide. We never saw it again. The other two boats were pulled up in a kind of controlled panic and Solomon, with a grin on his leathery face that I can still see today, strolled off in search of other quarry.

*

It was at about this time that another Grandma began to loom larger in our lives. Loom is perhaps not really the word, for she was thin to the verge of emaciation, bony and seemingly delicate (though as a soldier's wife she had survived hardships that would have carried off many a strong man). It seemed to me that she always wore a shawl whatever the temperature, a loosely knitted coffee-coloured affair which she perpetually held in place with her left hand. She was then about 70 and had been an army widow for thirty years. Her husband was Regimental Sergeant Major John Hewitt of the 24th Regiment of Foot—the South Wales Borderers. He had died in the Zulu War of 1879, with upwards of 900 comrades, when the 2nd Battalion was ambushed and wiped out under the shadow of Mount Isandhlwana in Natal. Unfailingly, every year on 22 January, my father reminded us that on this day there had died the soldier grandfather whom we never knew and whom, without difficulty, we had come to revere as our family hero. The difficulties presented themselves in later years. As was not unusual in those colonial-imperial times, John Hewitt's entire family was travelling with the regiment, or closely following it, throughout its various overseas postings; and my father's sisters knew, as he must have known, that when Grandfather Hewitt was killed he was no longer Regimental Sergeant Major. He was a private, and his career of drunkenness and misconduct had included the incredible distinction of having twice held, and lost, the rank of R.S.M. My father used to recall that as a boy of eight or nine in South Africa he was sent out daily to buy his father a bottle of Three Star brandy, which seldom lasted until evening. And he had seen his father, whose uniform and equipment as R.S.M. included a crook-handled walking-stick, take a morning parade by planting his feet wide apart, resting his clasped hands on the stick-handle behind his back, and thus converting himself into a drunken tripod skilled in not falling over. He must have led a charmed life. My brothers and I comforted ourselves, and sustained his cherished image, with the thought that such a record clearly showed him to have been recognized as a superb soldier. But I think he couldn't have

been all that good a father, and the rearing of the family de-
volved upon Grandma Hewitt and a succession of 'boys', or
coloured servants, in various parts of India and South Africa.

Grandma Hewitt at this time lived on her army pension in
a single room in Barclay Road, near Fulham Broadway and the
Eel Brook Common. In the recurring emergencies of my
mother's long terminal illness, she would come and stay with
us, as surrogate mum, for varying periods. And when she came,
she effortlessly but emphatically ruled the roost; and was
known to Harold and me (in the strictest secrecy) as The
Rooster. Born Mary Ann Robson in Manchester in 1848, she
had always taken a livelier interest in current affairs than most
other adults in my family circle. She was full of recollections,
and I often sought her company. On this ground my brother
Harold would sometimes accuse me of toadying. To him she
was an ogress. But she was worth cultivating, and I think
at that time she had a soft spot for me (in which I was supplanted, later, by Roland). She vividly remembered the 1861
American Civil War, and even the sailing of troopships from
Merseyside in the Crimean War in 1856. Palmerston, Disraeli,
and Gladstone were living memories for her. She rather tended
to speak of the Indian Mutiny as though she'd been in Cawn-
pore at the time; but although she was not in India until twenty
years after it was all over she could tell some interesting—
and some bloodcurdling—stories at second hand. We were
all vaguely proud that she had once been known and addressed
as Memsahib, and so was she. But her main influence upon me
was in the matter of books and reading.

In our house, reading silently round the fire was at this time
much the most popular of all relaxations. I have memories of
countless evenings on which five or six of us would be thus
absorbed, each with his own book, for two or three hours at a
time, the only sound being the sputtering of a tarry piece of
coal, the faint hissing of the kettle eternally on the trivet, or
the occasional popping of the gas-jet. I remember too with cruel
clarity the whirring of the hated mantel-clock as it cleared
its throat to strike my bed-time.

When Grandma Hewitt stayed with us, whether at Finsbury Park or at Fulham, I would go to the public library to get books for her two or three times every week. This was no hardship, and indeed no kindness or service, for I loved going into public libraries. I have never outgrown the initial wonder that it could be possible for a rather scruffy-looking boy of eight or nine to wander into those book-lined temples, browse all day if he wanted to, and actually take books home to read—all free of charge. Grandma Hewitt's reading soon began to influence my own. Of course she liked authors who wrote about India and the army: John Strange Winter (not even Grandma knew, at that time, that this was a woman), Maud Diver, Charles Lever in particular; but never Kipling, whom she simply would not read. I made the acquaintance of them all before I was ten, Maud Diver's *Captain Desmond V.C.* and *The Great Amulet* being the first grown-up books that actually gave me pleasure. A 'good' grown-up book at that time meant a book which all the adults commended to you but didn't seem to have read themselves: *The Pilgrim's Progress, Robinson Crusoe*, and *Hereward the Wake*, all unreadable. For children there was a gloomy spillover from the Victorians' lust for misery and melodrama, as in *Little Meg's Children, Christie's Old Organ*, and *The Wide Wide World*.

Above all, both Grandma Hewitt and my father wanted books about South Africa, and their authors were Rider Haggard (who still seems to me underrated), Olive Schreiner, and that prolific member of the astonishing Mitford clan, Bertram Mitford. There were contemporary novelists like the clerical brothers Silas and Joseph Hocking, George A. Birmingham, Stanley Weyman, Anthony Hope, Fred M. White, Robert W. Chambers, W. J. Locke the West Indian, and Jeffery Farnol. Marie Corelli was more revered in our home than Thomas à Kempis himself. Their books went through our household like a benignly infectious plague; and for some years it was our Grandma Hewitt who set the pace for us. She even persuaded me (but not my father) to read Mrs Emma Worboise, Mrs Henry Wood (I cried in bed over *The Channings*), Mrs Humphry

Ward, and Rosa Nouchette Cary. There seems to have been, though of course I was not aware of it then, a marked absence of authors such as Jane Austen, the Brontës, and Mrs Gaskell; and I was left to discover, and wallow in, Harrison Ainsworth, Mayne Reid, Scott, Dickens, and Thackeray for myself.

My father revered books and the bookish with a wistful appetite which (I can see this now) cried out for guidance from an 'adult education' mentor. He pinned his faith to a contemporary document known as 'Sir John Lubbock's Hundred Best Books'. This was a personal selection made public (I never knew why) by the then Lord Avebury; and it included nearly all the books that one didn't want to read, or gave up if one tried: Aristotle's *Ethics, The Koran,* Xenophon's *Memorabilia, The Niebelungenlied,* Schiller's *William Tell*; and it ended with 'Dickens's *Pickwick* and *David Copperfield'* (only) but 'Scott's novels' (apparently the lot). For the most part they were the books which, it seemed, you should expect to find in every intelligent man's private library; with, in most such libraries, their leaves uncut. But Sir John Lubbock himself had stirred my father's imagination with a book called *Marriage, Totemism and Religion*—the subject was greatly worrying him at that time, we were given to understand, and the book impressed him so much that he accepted without question the 'Lubbock Hundred'.

Grandma and my father disagreed (and I was on his side) about Edgar Wallace and his army stories, then having an immense vogue. Smithy and Nobby wᴄʳe very popular with us, while our military-minded Grandma sniffily rejected them as defamatory of the British Army. And, strange and sad to say, I had to part company with the grown-ups over P. G. Wodehouse, who burst upon us as early as 1909 with the school and cricketing adventures of Mike Jackson and Psmith, to hold us boys in thrall for the rest of our lives. Sometimes we came into possession, I simply can't imagine how, of a glossy periodical called *The Captain*, a huntin' shootin' Dornford Yates kind of magazine, edited by R. S. Warren Bell, which featured stories by Wodehouse and of which, today, a single copy would be worth a king's ransom. Bertie Wooster and Jeeves were yet to come, but from 1916 onwards Mr Wodehouse had no more ecstatic devo-tees, in all his long writing life, than Harold, Roland, and myself.

It was in discovering the literary tastes of my elders and betters, and especially in precociously trying to share them, that I first came to question the influence of the novelist on the minds of his readers. How could people read all these harrowing, frightening, wicked, and funny things without being morally tarnished, alerted to current social and political prob-lems, or attuned to the comic aspects of life that they never knew at first hand? Why was it that their daily conversation remained on so simple a level and that they dodged and depre-cated every attempt to raise it? Why, above all, did these avid readers, though here I exempted my father and Grandma Hewitt, seem to *know* so little? As for those two, my father might have known a lot, but he was both clever and dignified at ducking questions. You could never quite tell whether he knew the unspoken answers or whether they were not fit for young ears, but there were four encyclopedias in the house, he was a great looker-up, and there was always a respectful belief, or hope, that he had known the answer at once but was deter-mined to verify it rather than risk misleading us. Grandma, on the other hand, knew a bit about contemporary public affairs, but it seemed mainly to have been absorbed, and was exclusively expressed, in the kind of clichés and catch-phrases with which the Northcliffe Press was newly nourishing a readership that could be satisfied or fobbed off with outlines and jeering witti-cisms. Mr Asquith, to my Grandma Hewitt, was 'Old Wait-and-See'. I suppose he must have used the phrase in some nationally important context, but it clung to him as 'ninepence for four-pence' has clung to Lloyd George, 'You've never had it so good' to Mr Harold Macmillan, 'We are the masters now' to Lord Shawcross, and 'The pound in your pocket' to Sir Harold Wilson.

For the same kind of reason, Grandma Hewitt was a walking repository, rather than a dictionary, of clichés and catch-phrases;

and I have often wished she could have been known to Mr Eric Partridge during the compilation of his delectable dictionaries. Both she and I, and I'm sure my brothers, could pre-date many of Mr Partridge's attributions. Here are four examples, none of which he places earlier than 1945 and yet all of which were common currency in my Edwardian childhood: 'Just what the Doctor ordered', 'Are you kidding?', 'Cheats never prosper', and 'All behind like a cow's tail'.

And among the many other 'things my grandmother taught me' was the fabled significance of sneezing. 'Bless you!' she said whenever we sneezed, and no one else in our family—or, as I remember, in all our acquaintance—ever in those days said this or knew of any reason for saying it. I think it was she who told me that the priests used to say it during the Black Death, because a sneeze was the mortal symptom and the 'Bless you' a pious valediction to those about to die.

*

I find that there is in this period of my recollection, from my ninth birthday until somewhere near my eleventh, an almost total blank about school. I was sent to the LCC Elementary School in Kingwood Road, a turning off the Fulham Palace Road; and however I search my memory there come to light but two school episodes and two school personalities from the whole of this period.

The first episode, a trifling one, belongs fitly to the period. A teacher told me I had a Pears Soap smile which he thought 'untrustworthy'. I puzzled over this for years. The Pears Soap advertisements portrayed a number of widely differing faces. There was a sooty-looking tramp saying 'Thirty years ago I used Pears Soap, since when I've used no other'. There was a rather soppy-looking girl 'preparing to be a beautiful lady'. And there was a fat Pears baby reaching out of his bath after a cake of soap, of whom the caption said 'He won't be happy till he gets it'. Which of these had the untrustworthy smile? It put me against Pears Soap for many years.

I may have been unusually responsive, even romantic, about

the faces in well-known pictures. At Kingwood Road School
there hung in the assembly hall a framed reproduction of G. W.
Joy's oil-painting *The Bayswater Omnibus*. It depicts one side
of the interior of a horse-bus. Along the seat, backs to the long
window, are a worried-looking mother with a little girl and a
baby-in-arms (the latter, I decided, was being taken to hospital);
a beautiful lady with a parasol and a basket of flowers; a top-
hatted toff with spats, a rolled umbrella, and a newspaper;
and a uniformed nurse who is glancing up as a girl gets in
carrying a hat-box. Behind them all through the window (and
how the glass of those bus-windows used to rattle, without
breaking!), you could see the green of Kensington Gardens.
I must have gazed upon this picture so often and so long, during
prayers and other boring occasions in the hall, that it became
another world for me and I invented names, dispositions, and
life-stories for all the figures in it. This process was facilitated
at the time by the current republication, probably in the *Strand
Magazine*, of a Sherlock Holmes series, and by the imitative
habit of observation and brilliant deduction that everyone was
going in for.

The second Kingwood Road episode involved a Jewish boy
named David Blümberg, who became my particular friend. His
parents were Orthodox Jews, his father was German, his mother
I think Lithuanian; though I don't believe anyone would have
known he was Jewish if it hadn't been that every morning, at
'Scripture Lesson' time, he was allowed to leave the classroom
and read a book in the hall or in the playground. This odd-man-
out status is always unfair to a boy at a tough school, but if his
name is something like Blümberg and the political atmosphere
is that of 1910–14 he is surely marked down for an unhappy
time. Germany at that time was the popular enemy, German-
manufactured goods (inferior, we were always told, and imitative:
their famous trade-mark DRGM meant Dirty Rotten German
Make) were swamping the market; German airships were being
designed for war; German battleships were putting in provoca-
tive appearances at diplomatically sensitive places. All our
boys' weeklies, when they needed a bungling spy or a foreign

villain, used German ones. And once the Kaiser in a public speech had announced Germany's intention to find 'a place in the sun', the appearance of the German battleship *Panther* at Agadir in August 1911 was taken by everyone, especially the French and my Grandma Hewitt, to mean that the Germans were about to invade and annexe Morocco. I had no idea, of course, how close we then were to war, but anti-German feeling came near to hysteria, my friend David Blümberg was like a hunted animal and I was half afraid of being known as his buddy. Because we were inseparables, and because I was about twice his size, we were known as Mutt and Jeff, after two comic-paper figures of the period—tramps who befriended and upbraided each other in the manner of all cross-talk comedians. But although I must have looked big enough to defend him against aggression, his parents would never allow him to come out and play with me after school; they thought he was safer indoors.

I think the school had a high percentage of louts of whom I was always rather afraid. But there was one in particular who could, I suppose, have been regarded as the School Bully, and who would certainly have accepted the role proudly if it had been suggested for him. Oddly enough his name was Lemesne, though I don't know what French origins he may have had and his London accent was one of the least attractive, slurred, slovenly and glottal Cockney, all distorted vowels and wandering aitches. He was a heavily built boy, and his appearance was sufficiently frightening to ensure that every fight he undertook or provoked was a swift psychological walk-over. One day, in an unsupervised classroom interval between lessons, he suddenly accused the diminutive David Blümberg of stealing his pencil. I saw that he had David's arm twisted behind his back, heard his description of the trembling little boy as 'a bloody German Yiddisher thief', and angrily told him to lay off. He let the boy go and would have turned upon me but for the entry, at that moment, of the teacher. And during the next lesson he passed me a note saying that he would meet me 'under the arch' at ten past four.

Fighting in the playground had been recently forbidden. I can't now remember where the arch was, but it was a railway arch, and it certainly wasn't on my way home from school; and I am in no doubt that I was strongly minded to ignore Lemesne's invitation. He saw to it, though, that the proposed rendezvous was widely known about, and that the general anticipation was well fuelled. Lacking the courage to meet him at the railway arch, I lacked even more the courage to duck the encounter, go home, and face the universal derision of the next day—and, I guessed, of the future as far as one could see it. Moreover I could see by then that I should have to fight him sooner or later, or resign myself, as so many others had, to doing his bidding. It was my mini-Munich. So I went to the railway arch, and I clearly remember feeling as though I were walking in a dream—I must try to wake up and everything would be all right. I found about 15 or 20 boys waiting. They did not, I remember, look as though they were waiting for anything, especially anything dramatic or entertaining. They were all spinning tops or playing leapfrog or skylarking. But I knew why they were there, and at the sight of them, and of the waiting Lemesne, there took possession of me a sudden blinding ferocity such as I have never since believed possible. It was sheer panic transmuted into madness. I still find the recollection of it highly disturbing. Without a word to anyone I rushed at Lemesne, hitting out wildly with both fists, kicking his shins as he span round, beating and tearing and smashing away like a lunatic. If he expected some kind of preliminary Marquis of Queensberry sparring and dancing, he must have been grievously and memorably disappointed. What he got was an unannounced and murderous onslaught from a slightly younger boy, temporarily converted into a gibbering maniac, who could no more be stopped than a whirlwind. When he turned and ran I pursued him, banging the top of his head, kicking his behind when I could get close enough, until at last I overbalanced and fell, inevitably tearing out once more the much-mended knees of my breeches. He made good his escape. I never saw what happened to the crowd of boys. I remember that I was crying

with rage and I was probably slobbering. He avoided me always
thereafter, which did not matter. But he avoided David Blümberg too, which did.

I am sure that this ludicrous episode owed much, in the
excitement of its anticipation, to the crazy partisanship for and
against Jack Johnson, who in 1908 had become the first-ever
Negro world heavyweight boxing champion by beating the
French-Canadian Tommy Burns at Sydney, New South Wales.
This fight, which took place on Boxing Day, was stopped by
the police on the ground that Burns was likely to be gravely
injured. (Johnson was to hold the championship until 1915,
when at Havana he was knocked out by Jess Willard after no
fewer than 26 punishing rounds.) It is necessary, I think, to
have been a boy at that time to accept that a whole generation could have been so utterly obsessed with the fortunes
of one heavyweight slogger, but I think he was a symbol (absurd
as it must seem now) of black power, of the coming resurgence
of black peoples everywhere, and of the traditional British
hostility to slavery. His thirty years in the ring, and his 120
major fights, gave him some kind of heroic world stature with
the working classes in this country; but his defeat of the 'great
White Hope' Jim Jeffries at Reno in 1910 caused bitter disappointment and racial friction in America, where the
partisanship took the form of sectarian violence in many cities.
When Jack Johnson was signed up in England to meet Bombardier Billy Wells, a more popular boxing celebrity than any other
I remember, there was a most unusual development. The fight
was to be at Earls Court, on a site owned by the Metropolitan
District Railway. The American race riots had shocked the
world, and in England the lawyers conveniently remembered
that prize fighting, with or without gloves, with or without
observance of the Queensberry Rules, was unlawful. The Free
Churches, led by the Revd F. B. Meyer (a man greatly revered
by my parents), started a movement to get the contest banned
and to compensate its promoters by public subscription. Then it
was found that the compensation would amount to £12,000,
so the scheme had to be dropped. But someone persuaded the

Metropolitan and District Railway to restrain the lessee from permitting the fight; and at last it was off. There was fierce junior partisanship in Fulham, and (I gather) a feeling in the local pubs and clubs that the nation was going soft. Bombardier Wells was an object of much sympathy, but the prestige of Jack Johnson among the millions of vicarious pugilists attained greater heights than ever.

I have wondered, since, whether this preoccupation with strong men was the more widespread because children were, on the whole, a sickly and delicate lot. It seemed that in every group of children there would be someone wearing leg-irons because of rickets or poliomyelitis, someone with St. Vitus's Dance, someone with a hare-lip, someone with a dreadful squint, someone wearing a skull-cap on a head closely shaven because of head-lice or ringworm. Curable and preventable illnesses and afflictions of all kinds were accepted as incurable and non-preventable.

I do not remember that partisanship among the able-bodied led to any street violence in that period, though I believe there were factory-floor and barrack-room scuffles in cases where words were inadequate. It is therefore strange that, in the Fulham and Putney area, the one local and annual event which led considerable numbers of working-class men to rain blows upon each other was the Oxford and Cambridge Boat Race. This event has divided the British into Dark Blues and Light Blues ever since it became an annual contest in 1856 (it was started in 1829); but I doubt that the sale of blue lapel badges and streamers reached the same frenzied level anywhere as in Putney and Fulham when I was a boy. Almost everyone seemed to wear, on the Day, a light or dark blue enamelled lapel badge or button; and I knew of syndicates of boys who spread themselves out along the Putney-to-Mortlake towpath, not so much to watch the boat race as to solicit people's badges and buttons once it was over.

'Want yer badge any more Guv'nor?' 'Give us yer badge', they would wheedle; and, if their timing was right, they got badges by the score. Collectively they got badges by the thousand,

most of them being put away until the following year, for re-
sale to the boat-race public as if they were brand new. Today I
see my own share in this enterprise as one of the feebler commercial efforts in a signally uncommercial life, for although I
joined enthusiastically in the business of soliciting *post facto*
badges from riverside Oxford and Cambridge supporters, I gave
them away almost at once to boys who were collecting them
in greater earnestness, and who used large shopping bags for the
purpose.

Anyway the boat race was a Great Annual Event, sustaining
fierce antagonisms and much jeering, sometimes (indeed I think
usually) dividing families, sometimes leading to fights; and with
my co-urchins I always spent the whole day, with a packed
lunch, somewhere on the towpath between Putney and Hammersmith bridges. In 1912, on a cold and windy 30 March, both
boats filled with water and the Cambridge one sank. The
Oxford crew, to my great joy as one of their supporters, got
out in shallow water, emptied out their boat, and went on to
complete the course. Alas, the umpires decided that it was 'no
race'. It was re-rowed on 1 April and Oxford won by three
lengths. My brother Harold supported Cambridge, for no better
reason, I believe, than that his scholarship examination was
the 'Cambridge Junior Local'; and this sinking of the Cambridge
boat was eclipsed, for him, only by the sinking of the *Titanic* a
fortnight later.

The boat race was one of the few local occasions which, in
my father's eyes, might justify an unsupervised excursion so far
from home. It was no more than a couple of miles from our
house over Putney Bridge to the Putney-Hammersmith towpath,
the happiest playground of my childhood, the Mississippi river-
bank where I felt I was Tom Sawyer personified. I went there
without permission every weekend for years, the unspoken
assumption at home being that I was in the Bishop's Park—or,
more probably, playing in the street.

That very phrase evokes a dead time, a quiet that now seems
irrecoverable, shattered for ever by the motor vehicle. Children
of all ages used the roadway as a playground. Babies not yet

able to walk rested in the middle of the road while they decided which way to crawl next. Long skipping-ropes stretched right across while a dozen children skipped in attempted unison. Katharine Whitehorn wrote in *The Observer* of 26 March 1978: 'People . . . could play in the road, with occasional cries of "Car coming", and my mother's family played Badminton and left the net across the road all night.' Indeed, of the few vehicles that came along Gowan Avenue, most were hand-propelled: costers' barrows, bakers' and butchers' and milkmen's barrows, nearly always pushed from the wrong end so that, in places where the tradesman wanted to hurry, by using the barrow's centre of gravity he could support himself through giant strides and treble his speed, looking wildly funny as his legs dangled between touch-downs.

Our house was about equidistant from two big football grounds: Chelsea at Stamford Bridge and Fulham at Craven Cottage, whose teams were known respectively as the Pensioners and the Cottagers. Both grounds were and are in Fulham, Chelsea's Stamford Bridge being in fact at Walham Green, and Fulham's Craven Cottage being rather nearer to us. But for some reason my father was a Chelsea supporter. He always had a season ticket admitting two people to the covered stand, and on every possible Saturday during the football season he took my mother to Stamford Bridge. (We never, by the way, called her or thought of her as stepmother, and I resist the idea to this day.) She, most uncharacteristically, would get excited to the very verge of heart failure during a game; and must have been, after a few seasons, one of the very few mums in the country to understand the off-side rule in Soccer—which I certainly didn't until she explained it to me one day with salt and pepper-pots and egg-cups. Harold on Saturdays was usually playing football somewhere with his school, and I was always deputed to keep Roland amused—often with the parting assurance from my father: 'He will never forget you for this, you know', meaning (a) that I was in some way behaving nobly by not going off with my own friends and leaving my six-year-old brother alone in the house, and (b) that my father's conscience, though none too comfortable, was just not powerful enough to make him give up his Saturday football; or mother's either, I suppose.

But it was thus that Roland and I observed from the front-parlour window, on innumerable Saturday afternoons, the steady tramp of thousands and thousands of single-minded men along Gowan Avenue towards Walham Green if the important match of the week was at Chelsea's ground, or the other way towards Craven Cottage if it was at Fulham's. And on those days, and those only, there was an unbroken flow of one-way motor traffic, mainly taxicabs, hooting the trampers off the road and on to the footways. If it were not for Saturdays you could never have believed there were so many motor vehicles in the whole of the country. We came to recognize and to look out for individual taxicabs—they were nearly all Beardmores or Unics—for they were painted in bright colours such as emerald green, pale blue, and dark chocolate, which seemed somehow unsuitable, even then, to their sit-up-and-beg outline and design.

There were, however, Saturdays when my father was away on duty, and I was allowed to use the Chelsea season ticket with one of my pals. There were also Saturdays when Chelsea was 'away' and the Stamford Bridge ground could offer only the 'Chelsea Reserves' at play; and I could always have the season ticket then if I wanted it. But it says much for the magic of big names (Molyneux, Foulkes, Whittingham, Croal, Middelboe, one-eyed Thompson) that, little as I then knew about the crucial points of the game, in their absence I didn't much want to go. At the Fulham ground, Craven Cottage, boys from 9 to 14 years old could get in free for the last twenty minutes' play at any kind of match, and from about 1913 onwards I often did.

Never once in those five or six years, by the way, did I see or hear of any hooliganism in or near football grounds, however fierce the partisanship. Fierce it certainly was, and I remember how I would watch with astonishment and alarm the numerous excited stentors to be seen and heard at every match, roaring their anguished advice to the players and being themselves bellowed at by spectators who thought the advice offered was wrong. They all shouted through cupped hands, their eyes bulged, the veins in their necks stood out, and yet they never (to my surprise) actually exploded. My father called them unpaid referees and was far more tolerant of their behaviour than he sometimes was, I thought, of mine. His view was that most of them probably led harsh and drab lives, with little opportunity for letting off steam except at home, and certainly no chance of doing so at work, where a job could be so easily lost—and unemployment pay did not exist; and it was better that they direct the steam at a distant footballer than at their captive wives.

*

For some reason that I have never identified I had been pushed in at Kingwood Road School a year ahead of my rightful place on the ladder of learning. Consequently I was totally lost at everything except English. This may have been due to my father's tireless insistence that my brothers and I should speak our mother tongue according to the rules. He must have made us all sound educated, posh, and brainy. We weren't, and I was exceptionally stupid. His rules were firmly founded upon those laid down by a Mr Meiklejohn, in an English Grammar which occupied in our household a position usually accorded at that time to the Bible. Mr Meiklejohn was supported by *Pitman's Shorthand Dictionary* in all matters of pronunciation; and once you became adept, as I did at an early age under my father's eager tuition, in such use of phonetics you felt you simply couldn't go wrong. My father had never had time to acquire a regional accent. He was born (6 January 1869) in the Army Barracks at Eccleshall Bierlow, south-west of Sheffield, his father then being a Sergeant in the 24th Foot. Before he was of school age he was taken abroad with the regiment—I believe one of his earliest schools was in Gibraltar. Until he was ten years old he went to a variety of schools in India and South Africa—and sometimes, for longish periods, to no school at all, other than classes occasionally arranged by a garrison education officer. When his father was killed in the Zulu War he was brought home at the age of ten and sent as a boarder to the Duke of York's School for soldiers' orphans in King's Road, Chelsea, where of course he lived among a mixed collection of accents and dialects spoken by pupils and teachers alike. So he ploughed his own furrow. From my earliest recollection of him I can tell that his own speech was 'correct' beyond the point of pedantry, his pronunciations exactly obedient to the latest lexicographers' whims as they found their way into *Pitman* and, a little later, into *Nuttall's Standard Dictionary of the English Language*, based (it was proud to say on its title-page) *on the Labours of the most Eminent Lexicographers*. He made us say 'tordz' for towards and 'un-*toh*-ard' for untoward; we said 'de*sicc*ated' for *desi*ccated (no one else ever said this, and the modern *Nuttall* now follows the slovenly crowd). We knew the differences in pronunciation (a word itself we had to be *very* careful about) between frequent, absent, ferment, progress, and retail when they were used as adjectives and as verbs, and we were good on the contemporary pronunciation of words like privacy, complaisance, and despicable. And this often exposed us as oddities at school where, we found, the teachers knew less about pronunciation than our father and Messrs Nuttall and Pitman did.

We certainly lapsed from time to time, as most people will in the mild pursuit of popularity or to gain admission to a group. But if there was any spill-over from this at home, paternal correction was stern and instantaneous. You couldn't even do it as a feeble kind of joke. Once I was sent out to the street to ask the 'oil man' (a travelling horse-and-cart grocery and dry-goods shop which came along Gowan Avenue twice a week) for a packet of Cerebos Salt. 'E ain't got none.' I reported. 'Wot abaht sumfink else?' I must have been mad. It was worse than if I had poured out a torrent of four-letter obscenities; it sustained a changed father-and-son relationship for weeks. I didn't know at the time (I learned about it from the admirable Cousin Florrie) but my father even deplored the nursery rhyme 'Mary Mary quite contrary', on the ground that it taught children an incorrect pronunciation of 'contrary'. Years later I found that Mr Nuttall supported him, giving no alternative to '*con*trary' even when it meant captious; nor in its latest edition has it relented. But my Cousin Florrie, a teacher of English in LCC schools, both bewildered and delighted us boys by using colloquialisms like 'He does that rather well, don't he?' and 'She looks taller than him'. She bewildered us because to us she seemed immensely well-read and erudite, and I believe now that she was prompted to say these things by a mischievous amusement at my father's pedantry.

During the Finsbury Park years she had lived just round the corner from us, at No. 130 Hanley Road, and we had seen much of her and her teacher friends. They were young and up to date. I believe they puzzled my parents. Indeed some of them were little more than flappers—ah, there's a word on its way to oblivion: in those days it signified a teenage girl with her hair down, usually in a pigtail with a big bow. The bow flapped as she hurried about. A decade earlier, it seems, it had meant a young prostitute, but now the universal adoption of plaits and big bows had made it respectable, every girl from about fifteen upwards was a flapper, and the pillion seat on a motor cycle was known as a flapper-bracket. Cousin Florrie's flapper colleagues, probably I suppose young 'pupil-teachers', used catch-phrases which remain in my memory from the 1908–1915 period, and many of them are misunderstood and misused today. 'Don't you know?' is a perfect example. It has become a period 'silly ass' expression (Don't-yer-know?), probably clear enough in its original form to Dorothy Sayers but consistently misused by the actors who have played Lord Peter Wimsey and the producers who have failed to instruct them. I am quite sure that it meant 'You *must* know about that, surely?'; it was a semi-exasperated interjection in a narrative, used in conversation with a contemporary 'square' or fuddy-duddy and designed to save time by avoiding obvious detail. But nothing now will kill the belief that, as Marghanita Laski wrote in the *Times Literary Supplement* on 7 March 1968, 'the word "doncher" in "doncher know", "doncher think", stood for the pronunciation of the late Victorian and Edwardian silly ass or knut'. In my childhood it stood for exasperation and perplexity in the narrator, the implied silly ass being the listener who really didn't seem to know.

Similar expressions of the time were the inane 'I *don't* think', added to an opinion or a statement of intent to provide an ironical rejection of it—'He's a splendid performer, I *don't* think'; and 'That just goes to show'—which Eric Partridge dates no farther back than 1930!

But in Fulham, where we were seeing Cousin Florrie and her friends less frequently, she was gradually superseded, as a beneficent influence on my years of development, by three men (unknown to each other) who were about as dissimilar as Nature and nurture could have contrived. They need a chapter to themselves.

5

FULHAM FRIENDSHIPS

One of these men was Mr Herbert, and I find it astonishing, considering his lasting influence upon me, that I seem to know so little about him. I met him when I was eleven years old, and attached myself one day to a party of children in the Bishop's Park. He was in charge of them. They were all from the Sunday School at Munster Park Methodist Church, to which at that time I had never been, and Mr Herbert was their Sunday School teacher. They had been with him to see the Putney boathouses on the other side of the river, where the Thames Rowing Club and, at times, the Oxford and Cambridge University crews kept their skiffs. I was proudly sailing my model yacht, *The Sunbeam*, on the Bishop's Park lake and to my intense gratification they all crowded round to admire it. Finding that I knew one of the girls in the party, Mr Herbert invited me to join them in a picnic tea. It seemed to me an inspired suggestion. Then they all wanted to have tea on 'the sands', the artificial beach by means of which the benevolent Parks Committee had tried to make the place resemble the seaside. Mr Herbert was clearly determined that the picnic should be on the grass—the sand was said to be flea-ridden—and the occasion established him as a hero in my eyes for two reasons.

The first was the gentle and inexorable way in which he won them all round to picnicking on the grass; it involved something much more than just walking away with all the food, though I suppose that would have been enough. The second concerned our old enemy Solomon the park-keeper. Mr Herbert and two of the bigger boys had picked up a movable park bench and carried it about twenty yards to the spot chosen for the picnic. I think he wanted it as a kind of bar from which to dispense the sandwiches, buns and drinks, and, being a bit elderly for sitting cross-legged with the rest of us on the ground, also wanted some of it as a seat. Solomon arrived.

That there, said Solomon, was not allowed. What wasn't? Moving the park furniture. I was astonished, as we crowded round to listen, at this use of the word furniture in such a context, for I thought furniture was to be found only indoors. Mr Herbert told us all to sit down and get on with our tea, while he took Solomon by the elbow and coaxed him a few yards away. We could see that as he talked to Fulham's leading killjoy he was smiling and making conciliatory gestures, but we were quite unprepared for the bloodless victory which followed. Wonder of wonders, old Solomon suddenly nodded and walked away; and there were those among us who maintained that he looked almost happy, though they may have been misinterpreting some spasmodic rearrangement of the Solomon features.

Mr Herbert was a little man with white hair, bright blue eyes, and a rather yellow face—I suspect that he suffered from jaundice though it never occurred to any of us that he was ever unwell. He was a retired man, and I believe he had been a type-setter in the employment of William Willett, the printer, of Bow Lane in the City of London—the man who devised and finally (in 1916) induced the whole country and nearly the whole world to accept his Daylight Saving Scheme. Mr Herbert was a widower and had an unmarried daughter who was a piano tutor. But he had 'a way with children' that sets him apart from anyone else I have known and he was, I suppose, an eternal child himself, like J. M. Barrie or Lewis Carroll but, so far as I know, without their mixed-up sentiments. It was the custom of Sunday School teachers to arrange small excursions and outings, always quite separate from the big annual Sunday School Treat, for the children assigned to them as their 'Sunday School class'. Mr Herbert's little outings had become renowned, and (like a great many other Sunday scholars) I wanted to join them. This of course necessitated going to his Sunday School, and I caused some astonishment at home, followed by slightly sceptical approval, by announcing suddenly that I wanted to go. I was enrolled. The Sunday School was held in the church itself, girls downstairs, boys up in the long U-shaped gallery. When the full assembly had worked its way through a couple of hymns and a prayer, it stayed in the church but broke up into classes—groups of a dozen or so clustered round a teacher for 'biblical instruction'. What Mr Herbert's group then got was not biblical instruction but a vivid reading from something like *Treasure Island* or *The Settlers in Canada*. I don't know whether the Sunday School superintendent knew what was going on, but he may have refrained from enquiry because we were always the quietest group in the place.

Qualified thus as a member of the Herbert group, I was in a strong position to cadge from my parents the bus fares for the little excursions Mr Herbert arranged for his followers—to the Zoo, to Kew Gardens, to the British Museum, above all to the Natural History Museum at South Kensington. I had been collecting a series of cigarette cards depicting The Great Mammals, and had made the shattering discovery that their skeletons all seemed to be more or less distorted versions, big and little, of the human skeleton. It was going to be many years before I could read and understand Darwin: but my father, at that time a Free Church fundamentalist loyally antagonistic to all the works of the evolutionists, was unknowingly chipping away at his own authority by subscribing, on behalf of my brothers and myself, to Arthur Mee's *Children's Encyclopedia*. This was then coming out in fortnightly parts, and Harold and I fortnightly scrapped for the privilege of reading each number first. He usually won. Among a multitude of other exciting things, it expounded the Darwin theory in the simplest of language with no attempt at 'writing down'. The following (from Volume 8, page 5153) is typical:

Men had thought that species could not alter. They thought that for every species there had been a separate creation. They thought the remotest ancestors of cats had always been cats; that dogs had always been dogs, that wolves and jackals and hyenas had always been exactly as they are today; that all living things had descended from ancestors exactly like themselves.

Certainly, no one had thought they could have a common ancestry. At the Natural History Museum I asked Mr Herbert if we could try to find the skeleton of a sea-lion, which I had decided was the animal least likely to have a skeleton like mine. When I saw that its flippers were no more than a flexed upper arm and forearm, complete with all the phalanges as the fingers curled up into the armpit, and that its tail looked like a pair of legs pulled together, I was excited beyond all means of expression. And I had the sense even then to know that if I talked excitedly about this at home, the immediate result would be that Mr Herbert would be declared *persona non grata*. It was awe-inspiring to see the same kind of bone structure in the shrew mouse as in the diplodocus, 87 feet long from snout to tail. I was a bit young, perhaps, to have guessed that the first chapter of Genesis must be something for children, but I cannot remember that Mr Herbert expressed any view on the subject— even if I asked him. Harold knew more about all this than I did, but his reaction to it was pithily phrased years later (for both of us) by H. G. Wells in his *Experiment in Autobiography*: 'The human mind is as much a product of the struggle for survival as the snout of a pig, and may be as little equipped for the unearthing of fundamental truth.'

What Harold and Mr Herbert didn't know, and what even H. G. Wells seemed not to know, was whether the human eye, too, was 'a product of the struggle for survival'. I remember pestering people about this, and in particular my dear Cousin Florrie, who said that it was best sometimes not to enquire. It aroused some sympathy in the mind of my mother, to whom the eye was (she said) more of a miracle than anything else in the whole of nature. I learned many years later that Darwin himself thought it 'absurd in the highest degree . . . to suppose that the eye could have been formed by natural selection'. There have been no archaeologists' discoveries of embryo or half-formed eyes, no gradations from the simple to the complex, from monochrome vision to colour. In the depths of my dawning scepticism, I uneasily felt that the human eye was perhaps a special creation.

On the Day of the Diplodocus, I recall, Mr Herbert took us all home from South Kensington on a 'National' steam bus. Our minds switched from Natural History to the wonders of modern science. None of us had ever been on a steam bus before. Its steam was generated by heating water with a coal fire. There were steam-driven buses and Foden steam-waggons on the roads throughout my boyhood and adolescence, and I have often wondered how it could come about that they were ousted by the more costly and wasteful internal combustion engine. I suppose they may come back again. The first motor cars back in the 1880s were steam cars, and their drivers were called chauffeurs because they used to stoke the fires producing the steam. The 'National' buses always moved off smoothly and silently, but I remember that stopping often involved a con-siderable jerk. And yet the jerk can't have been as violent as I seem to remember, for the speed of all motor vehicles along the Fulham Road, and, no doubt, many similar roads, was at that time limited by law to ten miles an hour. The steam buses were supplanted by the lumbering old petrol-driven 'Vanguards', whose back wheels were set so far forward (to achieve a small turning circle) that on steep hills one or two of them were actually tipped up by passengers crowding on the stairs as they waited to get off.

It was scarcely less exciting to be taken on the London County Council's electric trams. These had been running along the Fulham Palace Road and over Putney Bridge since 1909; and when Mr Herbert took us to Putney Heath for picnics and games he sometimes piled us all on to a tramcar as, I suspect, a part of the fun—we could easily have walked and, when not with a Mr Herbert party, I often did. Of course we all went on the top deck and hurried to the front end, which overhung the bogey-wheels by about eight feet and accordingly swayed about at the corners like a rudderless boat in a storm. Inevitably somebody was sick, an event made all the more likely by the ever-present stale reek of cheap tobacco. I came to recognize the musty pungency of Faulkner's Nosegay Shag, and to marvel that it could be thought qualified for such an evocative name.

A current joke was that few people could afford to be sick on a tramcar, since it 'cost forty bob to spit'. There were two kinds of printed injunction about spitting on trams, and I think their appearance on the vehicles may have been separated by a year or two. The first said, 'In the interests of cleanliness and the prevention of consumption, passengers are kindly requested to abstain from the objectionable and dangerous habit of spitting.' I can't remember whether it outlined what would happen to a passenger who, nevertheless, spat. Nor, incidentally, could I ever understand why anybody spat at all, on or off tramcars, or why there were spittoons in places like pubs to encourage their marksmanship. The more politely persuasive of the two tramcar notices must have been deemed ineffective, for it was soon supplanted by another, slightly larger but terser, which said sternly, DO NOT SPIT: PENALTY 40s. And yet I never saw anyone spit on a tramcar, though I watched for it excitedly whenever I had the chance.

It was in the company of Mr Herbert and his Sunday School following that I made my second visit to a cinema. (The first had been in my mother's arms at about the age of twelve months.) Since then, I had grown accustomed to the marvels of the magic lantern: first, through visits to Wally Gerrard's house, where a magic lantern was one of the attractions, and from about 1908 onwards through our own acquisition of an Army and Navy Stores magic lantern, price 92 shillings and sixpence with eight slides. Four slides told the story of a London Fire Brigade hero called Bob the Fireman. It seems odd to me that the second cinema visit, after a lapse of nine years, should (in contrast with the first) have left in my mind virtually no record of what was shown on the screen. The explanation probably is that I was absorbed in the mechanics and showman-ship of the whole thing. In the Fulham Road near the Fire Station a shop had been converted into a tiny cinema, though that is not what it was called. It was called the Parsons Green Moving Picture Theatre; and it seems a happy thought that the wonder and the magic of 'moving pictures', even then probably twenty years old and yet growing year by year, should sustain the word 'movie' in our language to this day. (Not that we ever used the word then: I believe its public admission to un-American English happened in Bernard Shaw's *Heartbreak House* towards the end of the war.) I suppose the Parsons Green Moving Picture Theatre seated an audience of thirty at the most, the front three rows of chairs being very small ones of the kind seen in nursery schools, and behind those (for the grown-ups) there were padded forms with no backs to them. Saturday performances started at 3 p.m. and the price of admission was twopence-halfpenny.

The music was provided by an old horn-type gramophone, operated by the ticket cashier, its horn protruding through a hole cut in the wall of the box-office. The films were all very short, and no doubt very old—they broke down many times in each performance. And at each breakdown a stout lady who always sat on a cushioned stool near the Exit (it was the first time I ever saw the word Exit, and to this day I don't understand why it is better than Out) tugged at a little chain hanging from the gas-lamp near the door and, it seemed to our startled eyes, flooded the room with dazzling light. Mr Herbert told us that the management had learned not to leave a company of children in the dark with nothing to engage their attention. An audience of grown-ups were allowed to wait in the dark, I believe, during breakdowns. But they probably knew how to pass the time.

It was I think a year or two after that (probably 1912) when my parents first took us all to the newly opened Putney Bridge Kinema: a splendid edifice, we thought, with a domed entrance; two or three hundred seats; a curtain that pulled itself, with an unforgettable swish, across the screen at the beginning and end of each picture—it bore corrugated references to what we had just seen and what was to come next; a little string ensemble eked out by an indefatigable pianist; and brown-uniformed attendants who paraded the aisles from time to time squirting deodorant over our heads (I wonder why?). The lights went up at the end of each picture, and it was then that the attendants began shouting 'Sway out please' and 'Cigarette, Choc*leet*'.

The very first time we were taken to this stately pleasure-dome, and waited while my father paid our admission fees, I leaned over and whispered in five-year-old Roland's ear the mysterious words he must have been hearing so often from me in recent months: 'Moving pictures!' He tells me that once he was inside, and seated on his father's lap, he noticed that there were indeed pictures all round the walls, and he was waiting breathlessly for them all to start moving when, to his intense disappointment, all the lights went out. It was some time before he found that everyone else was now looking at a huge illuminated square at the end of a searchlight, and even longer before he was prepared to allow that the flickering figures to be seen on it must be the moving pictures for which I had so long and so excitedly prepared him.

Visits to the Putney Bridge Kinema became a weekly occurrence, and it was there that we saw our first Charlie Chaplin film. It was called *Laughing Gas*, and it established a devoted family of Chaplin addicts who were never, in the next seventy years, to waver in their loyalty. The universal Chaplin impact was something I shall never really understand. For years it seemed to me that there are so many totally humourless people in the world that success on the Chaplin scale simply shouldn't be possible, that it is a phenomenon calling for some transcendental explanation. Then I saw that this point of view merely rationalizes the feeling, in the breast of each individual Chaplinite, that Chaplin really belongs to him alone, that there is no one else who *quite* understands just how funny life can be. I do not see how this universal act of identity could have survived Charlie's ham sociological period, his *City Lights* and his *Great Dictator* and *Monsieur Verdoux* and the rest. But when I was a boy no one could have foreseen those aberrations.

Three actresses of the time enslaved us, and at that age I was precociously ready for enslavement: 'eleven-plus' was for me, I now realize, a prominent emotional milestone. They personified our more ecstatic dreams of the fair: Mary Pickford, Daphne Wain, and Pearl White. Miss White held us by reason of the terrifying predicaments we always had to leave her in. As the curtain swished across at the end she was always crying for help from a seventh-floor window in a burning building, hanging by her beautifully manicured fingernails from the outside of a balloon basket, or bound and struggling gracefully in the path of an express train. Her films bore titles like *The Exploits of Elaine*, and it was only the need that she should survive for at least one more advertised Exploit that sent us home partly optimistic about her future. Mary Pickford and Daphne Wain held us by their beauty, whatever kind of story it had to illuminate, and they usually got their stories over in one go.

Those cinema-going days are dramatically linked in my memory with the theme of 'playing in the street' because one Friday evening, after some doubtless infuriating offence against paternal discipline, I was told to go to bed while the rest of the family went off to the Putney Bridge Kinema for the evening. I suppose it reveals something about my good father's state of desperation about me that he should have decided at such a time to leave me, as a boy of ten or eleven, in the care of our poor old maid-of-all-work, the stone-deaf Annie. It was a fine summer's evening. I had absolutely no intention of staying indoors while it was daylight, and from the street I could hear the yells of Cowboys and Indians. There was little hope of getting to the front door past the watchful Annie, whose deafness had sharpened all the other perceptions with which you normally monitor the behaviour of the young; and even if I did, I had no street door key with which to let myself in when the time came to return home.

So I went out on to the balcony and slid down one of the pillars. Annie neither saw me go nor, it seems, looked into my bedroom at any time to make sure that I was still there. I must have supposed that climbing the pillar at the close of play would present no problems, but it presented the problem that I simply couldn't do it. Friendly hands giving me a bunk-up did no more than enable me to grasp the balcony railings, but I had no confidence in their capacity to remain in position while I hauled myself up and over them. We had always been warned that we were not to lean on them, or indeed to go out on to the balcony at all. Down on the ground again, hot, panting and nearing defeat, I was told by a boy called Albie Marsh that his father had a ladder lying in their front garden. We all dashed off to get it, and the ensuing procession of ladder-bearers was seen by I don't know how many of the interested neighbours, many of whom were gossiping at their gates because the heat indoors was stifling. In the event I got back into the bedroom without mishap, all unobserved by Annie, and the ladder was duly returned to base.

I set it down to my father's credit that, although he soon got to know about this escapade, he pretended not to know. Of course it may be that he privately approved, however grudgingly, of his urchin son's enterprise and determination, but it seems more likely that he simply didn't know what next to do about me. And though I long suspected that this or that neighbour had spoken about the ladder, my mother eventually told me that I had left tar-stained bootmarks on the balcony and, worse, on the bedroom floor. In that sweltering summer of 1911 our recently macadamized road surface in Gowan Avenue, of which at first we had been so proud, had turned into a shimmering expanse of viscous tar. Horse traffic couldn't use it for some days, and at intervals along the road workmen had spread gravel paths to make dry pedestrian crossings.

On 19 August 1911 the shade temperature at Greenwich was 100 degrees Fahrenheit, the highest recorded in Great Britain, they were saying, for forty years. Because it was still unthinkable to walk the streets bare-headed, even for the poorest people, and whatever the weather or the temperature, 1911 became The Year of the Straw Hat. The normally universal cloth cap was far too hot, and every male who could afford one (and was more than about fifteen years old) wore a straw 'boater'. I longed to have a boater, but had to wait some years for it. Its disadvantage was that, unlike a sombrero, it was not fitted with a chinstrap to hold it on in a high wind; instead you had to buy a 'hatguard', a little spring clip attached to a black cord, the clip fastening on to the hat-brim and the cord being secured in a jacket button-hole. Everyone knew that if a high wind blew off a straw hat thus secured, the jerk at the end of the cord would probably snap the hat-brim. But the cord looked important and dressy, like the silk cord securing pince-nez; and it was favoured by the 'knuts', that is to say the flashy young men of the time. Among the non-flashy, there was a certain shyness about wearing the first straw hat in spring: one watched anxiously from front-room windows for the first glimpse of some such pioneer.

It was during the tremendous heat of August 1911 that my revered Mr Herbert had a stroke (as, I believe, did many elderly people) and disappeared from our scene for many months. I do not remember that he played any active part in my life after that. I wonder if he knew (I wish I could be sure he knew) that he opened my mind far more than any of the harassed and baffled teachers in my various schools, and taught me to think and question.

Mr Herbert had one peculiarity: he would never go on an Underground railway, much as we all sometimes begged him to take us. The Underground was by no means a novelty; the Metropolitan Railway, underground for most of its track, had opened in 1864, the City and South London (which dived under the River Thames) in 1890, and until 1901 all their trains were pulled by steam engines. Accordingly they were covered in soot—I can remember that my father had a pair of brown leather gloves whose palms and fingers had been blackened by the door-handles of Underground trains. Mr Herbert, I believe, thought that if there were an accident in one of the tunnels—a derailment, a collision, or a fire—there could be absolutely no escape for anyone. If our parents cared to take us down there, well and good. He would take no such responsibility. I think he must have been unusual. When the President of the Board of Trade (it was Mr Lloyd George) opened the Charing Cross and Highgate Tube in 1907, 127,500 people availed themselves of the free travel it offered them for one exciting day.

My parents can have had no such inhibitions either, for I have very early recollections of the various Underground railways—all electrified by 1902—and of their biscuit-coloured basket-work seats, their swaying straps, the constant smell of hot metal from (I supposed) the 'live rail', and the shouts of the guards—one guard to every other carriage.

It was two London railwaymen of the Underground who shared with Mr Herbert the doubtful distinction of shaping my life during the Fulham years. One was Jim Elderkin, whom I have already mentioned. The other was Arthur Wheeler. And it's a strange coincidence that both were foster-children (neither of them, I think, formally adopted)—Jim of my Grandma Speed and Arthur of my stepmother during her first marriage. Jim was a guard on the District Railway, Arthur a signalman on the Central London. Arthur regarded Jim with a disdain that must have been based on something more than the difference between a signalman and a guard, but to my brothers and me they were both indulgent and generous. None of us ever knew where they came from, but both were utterly devoted to their adoptive parents and both very good to us boys, so much younger. Jim's position as one of our patron saints was assured from the moment he bought himself a Decca portable gramophone. That is to say, he must have thought he was buying it for himself, unprepared for the way in which his vulnerable good nature would expose him to our take-over methods. He came to our house with it one Saturday evening because he wanted my father's advice on the buying of records; and my father, as a bandsman and an orchestral flautist, was an authority on all the popular classics.

I cannot forget the moment when Jim proudly placed his new acquisition on our back-parlour table, an enigmatic object on the brown velvet bobble-edged tablecloth, and looked at all our faces to make sure that we were suitably ready for what he was about to reveal. While it was closed it looked like the carrying-case of a modern portable typewriter, perhaps a rather fat one. He opened it to display a ten-inch turntable, a silver-coloured soundbox and a tone-arm which, while the lid was held in position by a hinged lid-stay, discharged its inexplicable torrent of music into the circular metal dish, bright and shining, which transformed the upturned lid into an echoing sound-chamber. Among us all my father seemed the least impressed at this stage. It may have looked all right, he seemed to be thinking, but he expected nothing much in the way of sound reproduction. We had all heard the early gramophones—they began life as 'phonographs', they played cylindrical records that looked like shiny black jampots, and they were introduced by way of an adenoidal voice saying 'Edison Bell Record'. The noise that followed, usually singing, was truly awful. Living at that time in Walham Green was my mother's Uncle Will, a prosperous funeral director, who seemed to possess most of these modern marvels (a few years later he had, for example, a Chappell pianola). His phonograph had an immense gold-coloured horn for the emission of its excruciating sounds; and among these was the first mechanically reproduced music I had ever heard. This machine led, I remember, to a temporary coolness between my father and Uncle Will, for the record played to us was a song called *The Cocky Olly Bird*—this was how it was described on the label. My father insisted that it was a misunderstanding of Cock Yolly Bird, an ancient pet-name (meaning 'dear little bird') revived during the Boer War as a nickname for Australian troops, who wore 'Cock Yolly' feathers in their hats. My father regarded himself as an authority on everything South African.

My first experience of band music had been provided by the so-called 'German Bands' which played in the streets for money, and by Salvation Army bands. No one could ever tell me why the former were called German Bands. My father stoutly maintained that their members were all Germans (as, I suppose, at one time they may have been); and he scorned them because, he said, their trombones were equipped with stops instead of slides, a difference that seems to have been a bit like the one separating a piano-organ from a Blüthner concert grand. But I remember one band in the Stroud Green Road that turned out to be deeply versed in native Cockney obscenities if you threw conkers into the bells of its instruments during performances. The street-corner Salvation Army bands, which played hymn tunes and not marches, may not have been much good but they were good enough to whet my juvenile appetite for what a good brass band *could* do.

We had a Hurlingham and District Military Band ('military' meaning of course that it had a wood-wind section), and it practised one night a week at the Borough Council's Transport Depot in Munster Road—on condition that it would give *free* performances in the Council's parks during the summer season. You could hear it at practice from outside the building, but sometimes it was possible to get in and stand quietly in a corner for an hour or so. I got in because I knew Mr. Yellowlees, the tenor trombone, a blacksmith whose smithy was in Dawes Road and who would always, on a suitable day, repair an iron hoop for nothing. I don't know why, but I have nearly always preferred rehearsals to finished performances. It may be that it has satisfied my longing to be 'one of them', to be a real musician instead of just 'musical'.

The first records that Jim presented to us were a couple of military marches called 'Under the Double Eagle' and 'Belphegor', plus a sugary composition called 'Hearts and Flowers'. To our unprepared ears the quality of the reproduction was simply astounding. My father was incredulous, converted at once, his enthusiasm such that he—and we—began drawing up lists of the records we would like to hear. Among them was Auber's *Crown Diamonds* Overture, whose long and lovely flute introduction my father had practised at home ever since I was a baby. Jim, who knew nothing about music and never made any progress, became nonetheless a willing and slavish victim of our exploitation, arriving every Saturday evening with new orchestral and band recordings of the well-known overtures, suites, marches, and operatic 'arrangements' and selections whose names we all pressed upon him. I suppose he was shockingly victimized, but he never seemed to mind and he was instrumental in laying the foundations of our musical experience. Instrumental, did I say? He laid it. Those were Saturday nights of sheer ecstasy, longed for all the week; and never since, among the superb reproductions of modern hi-fi technology or even in any concert hall, have I been so excited and engulfed by the power of music. The majority of the records were trade-marked Columbia, His Master's Voice, Scala, Regal, and Zonophone, their prices varied from one shilling and sixpence to eight shillings, and for 'celebrities' like Caruso and Tetraz-zini you had to be content, which I never was, with a single-sided record.

One complication was that my father declared every record-ing to have been played too fast, and we had to slow it down or he wouldn't keep quiet. On those early machines you could vary the speed, but if you did you also varied the pitch. Accor-dingly we got used to hearing *Zampa, William Tell, The Merry Wives of Windsor,* and *Rosamunde* played in a lower key than everyone else seemed to think proper; and because I was always able to carry in the musical memory the exact pitch of any composition known to me, it always seemed in later years at concert halls that the performers were making the very mistakes my father had unfailingly condemned, blowing and scraping away like madmen.

And it was Jim who introduced me to the music hall, a pro-cess which involved deception at home. I forget what the pretence or deception had to be, but my mother in particular would never have allowed me to go into a music hall. I had never been inside a theatre, not even to a pantomime. I had wondered why we were taught at school to revere the plays of Shakespeare but were not allowed to see them performed in the places built for them. I pon-dered about the play-titles on the hoardings and on the sides of buses. Martin-Harvey in *The Only Way, Are you a Mason?, The Blue Bird*; there must have been something sinister or indecent about these. A young woman who lived across the road had given a song and dance at a Scouts' concert (we were not there) and a neighbour told my mother in a low voice that she had 'tights right up to her thighs'. Harold and I thought they wouldn't have been very interesting any lower down, but we had come to understand how it was that there were Two Worlds, to be acknowledged and talked about only on rigidly separate occa-sions and in separately recruited company.

I simply could not understand what could be evil about a hall with music in it. I did understand that the music halls had bars where you could drink during the intervals or (if you preferred it) throughout the evening; and my mother had sad memories of what drunkenness had meant to some of her childhood friends. It was her belief, and Grandma Speed's, that the theatre and the music hall were mere devices for encouraging people to drink. Charlie Chaplin records in his autobiography that every music-hall entertainer, after his act, was expected to go to the bar and drink with the customers—and would get no further engagements if he didn't. Many of the Fulham pubs advertised 'musical evenings', and those with gardens made a special feature of open-air concerts in summer. My mother thought this was where a great number of young people began a lifetime, usually a short one, of drunkenness. And she was probably right.

But the music hall, having begun as a sing-song in a pub, had already become the Palace of Varieties, and its progress from drunken knees-up to theatrical respectability was nearly complete. Charles Booth had written as early as 1889 in his *Life and Labour of the People in London* that 'the story of progress in this respect may be traced in many of the existing places which, from a bar parlour and a piano, to an accompaniment on which friends "obliged with a song", have passed through every stage to that of music hall; the presiding chairman being still occasionally, and the call for drinks in almost every case, retained. But the character of the songs on the whole is better, and other things are offered: it becomes a "variety" entertainment.' In 1912 King George V decreed (or perhaps merely acquiesced in) the first of all the Royal Command Performances. But if this was intended as the music hall's final accolade of respectability it was not so regarded in our house, and indeed it may well have been that the reputation of royal households was such that even a King of England couldn't decree anything into respectability.

By 1911 the 'presiding chairman' was a thing of the past; and for my part, far from being seduced into drunkenness, I never even saw the bar. (Jim was a non-drinker.) I think the biggest surprise of my first music-hall visit—at the Hammersmith Palace of Varieties—was the orchestra. I was accustomed by this time to the sound of a band or orchestra tuning up, and to me it has always been a strangely pleasant and exciting cacophony, full of mouth-watering promise and chaotic splendour. The orchestra at the Hammersmith Palace spent less time over this than I had expected, but it was still effective enough as a musical aphrodisiac. And then it played! Its speed was ludicrous, maniacal, contemptuous. The raucous 'Overture' lasted about thirty deafening seconds and ended with an irrelevant crash of cymbals. I was extremely disappointed and scornful, but I was to discover that all music-hall orchestras did it; and that, indeed, these places were not halls of music but theatres where entertainers told funny stories, enacted funny sketches, abused each other, conjured, juggled, contorted themselves, sang and danced, performed highly dangerous acrobatics and—very occasionally—played popular classics on piano, violin, trumpet, or mouth-organ. I thought they were all utterly enchanting.

Fred Karno was then at the height of his fame as producer of the 'Birds' series of comedy sketches—*Early Birds, Jail Birds, Mumming Birds*, and others; and on these he constructed a huge theatrical empire of over thirty companies, fostering such outstanding performers as Charlie Chaplin, George Graves, Harry Weldon, and Billie Reeves. On that first evening at the Hammersmith Palace we saw Bransby Williams in a series of the impersonations for which he was renowned—Uriah Heep, Micawber, and the Abbé Liszt. In the last-named, for some reason, he staggered about the stage playing a concertina, and someone in the gallery threw a coin on to the stage. A dropped coin in those days made a bright and unmistakable ringing sound. Bransby Williams stopped playing. 'That', he shouted, 'is an insult, and I'm not accustomed to insults.' I was petrified. He strode off the stage to cries of 'Come back Bransby', 'Come on mate, get on with it', 'Good old Bransby', etc. And after a while, encouraged no doubt from off-stage, he graciously came back to complete his act.

On other Saturday evenings in those exciting years I was taken to the Granville at Walham Green, the Putney Hippodrome and Shepherds Bush Empire, seeing the same variety artistes (as they liked to be called) time after time: Ernie Mayne, Sam Mayo, T. E. Dunville, Ernie Lotinga, and a host of less famous names. I have before me a Granville Theatre of Varieties programme for 18 August 1911, in which Fred Karno presented 'Mumming Birds', with a caste including the now forgotten names of Fred Arthur, Wheeler and Wilson, The Martins, Terry and Birtley, Arthur Clifton, Madoline Rees (most of whom I saw on other occasions) and 'The Cinematograph Showing New Pictures'. Seats in the Orchestra Stalls cost one shilling, Pit Stalls ninepence, Circle sixpence, Gallery threepence. 'Mumming Birds' was the mildly bawdy sketch in which, three years earlier, Charlie Chaplin had played, at the age of eighteen, the part of a comedy drunk in a highly individual way that ensured his future and his fortune. But I never saw Charlie Chaplin on the stage.

I remember being astonished at the coarseness and the sexual innuendos of T. E. Dunville and Sam Mayo; I could outdo them both (I believed) in suitable company, but it was probably because of them and their imitators that, while I was uncomfortable when female artistes were on the stage (I suppose I didn't like to think they had to associate with the Dunvilles and the Mayos), I positively hated the females who impersonated males, the Vesta Tilleys and the Hetty Kings. I was unable to see why all comedians couldn't be as unembarrassing as Billy Merson. I never saw pantomimes until I took my own children to them, and even then they were spoiled for me by the transvestite principal boy and pantomime dames, theatrical eccentricities I have simply never understood. To this day Danny La Rue, gifted as I'm sure he must be, makes my flesh crawl. George Robey was reputed to be the supreme pantomime dame, but his double handicap was that I regarded him anyway as a self-satisfied bore. And although I saw Harry Lauder only once, I thought him a bore too: his success and réclame have always mystified me.

Now I felt certain that my growing addiction to the music hall would be frowned upon not only by my parents but also by Mr Herbert. Mr Herbert, therefore, must not be allowed to know and my life was becoming complicated. And although this involved none of the deception practised upon my parents, for there was absolutely no reason why I should tell Mr Herbert, today I find it strange that I felt more conscience-smitten about him than about them in relation to it. A recurring nightmare was the fear that I might get caught by one of them listening to someone like Nellie Wallace. But then came the day of the fish supper in Sam Isaacs.

Sam Isaacs was at that time the Harrods of the fish-and-chips world. Sam had many shops and his fish and chips, which cost a little more than you had to pay in those lesser shops with the marble-topped tables (Sam gave you a white tablecloth), were generally considered to be worth a lot more. I believe I am writing about the very conception and birth of this vast industry, soon to replace the Roast Beef of Old England as our distinguishing national meal; and I can certainly remember, from about 1908 onwards, a growing habit of walking along the king's highway eating a pennyworth of chips from a piece of newspaper supported on the palm and outstretched fingers of one hand. In 1889 W. C. Morrow had prepared us for the phrase when he wrote, in his book *Bohemian Paris*, about 'fried potato women serving crisp brown chips'; but I suppose it is obvious that, when you are frying large quantities of fish for sale and want to serve it with a convenient vegetable that will also fry, the potato is an unbeatable candidate. But it won't fry unless you cut it into strips or flakes.

There was a Sam Isaacs shop within a few doors of the Granville Theatre of Varieties at Walham Green, and it was in there—I think early in 1912—that Jim Elderkin treated me to my first sit-down meal of fish and chips. It ranks in my memory above any banquet I have ever worked my way through. Years later in my teens, any evening at a music hall, theatre, or cinema was incomplete without the fish-and-chips finale. But the almost unbelievable sequel to that first Sam Isaacs supper was that on the following Sunday, during one of my diminishing attendances at Sunday School, three boys told me they had seen me going into the Granville as they were coming out from an earlier performance (there were three on Saturdays), and that their host for that evening had been Mr Herbert! I suppose something incurably furtive in my character is revealed by the fact that, even then, I didn't tell Mr Herbert that I had been to the Granville, and fatuously hoped he wouldn't know.

If I were asked to say what kind of music-hall turn remains in my memory as archetypal and is most sadly to be missed, I should name the 'comedy duo', the cross-talk act between comic and stooge which usually ended with a dance in which they moved in almost perfect and, it seemed to me, miraculous unison. I used to watch that final dance in utter astonishment that two human beings could so nearly synchronize every tiny movement of heads and limbs, ending with their strutting exit as they removed and twiddled their straw boaters or opera hats. I find that the dominant emotion they left in one's mind, as the applause followed them into the wings, was *gratitude*. I felt then, and have felt ever since at any public performance which has 'stopped the world' for me, that my own applause must convey affectionate gratitude rather than the conventional praise, admiration, and encouragement.

At some time in 1913 my parents for some reason transferred their allegiance from the chapels we had usually attended at Walham Green and Munster Park (always in the evenings) to a newly built Congregational Church in Fulham Palace Road. Its interior was all unadorned red brick and polished light oak and angularity. It was no doubt ahead of its time in this kind of starkly functional austerity and it seemed to me to represent a new sort of religion in which there could be no place for such as my Mr Herbert. In the nonconformist churches then the personality and in particular the eloquence of the Minister was all-important. The Fulham Palace Road Minister was a white-haired Mr Shirley, whom my father greatly admired for his evangelistic oratory. 'Shirley was magnificent this evening', he would say on the way home, and we would all agree that

Shirley had been magnificent. I sometimes feel a kind of humiliation when I realize that, among all the great Free Church preachers I have heard, including F. B. Meyer, Dr Horton, Dinsdale Young, Ernest Rattenbury, Dr Fort Newton (of the City Temple), I remember no single word, no message, no challenge to the mind except one apocalyptic pronouncement from Mr Shirley in 1914. He said that in a Christian world a war with Germany would be impossible, unthinkable, and yet such a war was now clearly coming. I don't remember what Christians were expected to do about that. Pray, probably. But the sermon frightened me out of any belief that war could be heroic or splendid or rewarding or in any conceivable way justified. War was suddenly on top of us, and at close quarters you could see that in real life it was cruel, filthy, and mad.

6

THE KAISER'S WAR

I have always thought of the two World Wars as the Kaiser's and Hitler's, identifying each man as a kind of narcissistic chump being fattened by millions upon millions of dupes for the part of the mad proxy king. So I shall be speaking here of the Kaiser's War. I was twelve years old when it began; and for perhaps eighteen months before that I had been acquiring, as if by accident, a superficial knowledge about the doom-laden trend of current affairs in a way that must, I think, have been unusual. I was learning Pitman's shorthand on the 'Commercial Side' of a London County Council Central School syllabus. My father, who had taught himself, had been proficient at it for more than ten years, and he now welcomed the household presence of a newly kindred spirit. For I loved shorthand as a kind of secret language and, through him, had known the rudiments of Pitman's since I was about seven years old. Now, said my father, we would develop our skill together and work up our speed. It was an exciting new relationship, for I had felt in recent years that he had written me off as a street urchin, a method of wearing out clothes and footwear and parental goodwill, and a member of the grey mass of the non-studious who failed examinations.

At every opportunity he sat with me at the back-parlour table to coach me through an hour's shorthand dictation. He took the *Daily Telegraph, The Times, The Referee*, or *John Bull*, usually the last-named, and patiently marked off the words of an article in hundreds, putting a red-ink stroke after every hundredth word. My mother was called in, whatever else she might want to be doing, to read aloud to us the passages thus marked, perhaps 500 words in ten minutes; and she started and stopped us by watching also the second hand of a loudly-ticking alarm clock on the table in front of her. I can remember him saying that 500 words in ten minutes was of course 'very childish' but that I should soon improve. And he was right. We were soon doing 500 in five minutes, and at one time, early in the war and shortly before we moved away from Fulham, we had got up to 500 in three minutes, and that is a speed (166 words a minute) which I have never attained since and which now seems to me impossible.

It was in the course of these shorthand exercises that I became familiar with words and phrases which had no special meaning for me then but which I could turn to what I hoped was impressive use later. The Schlieffen Plan, the *Entente Cordiale* (my father told me to write Entente as ontong), the Balkans, the Triple Alliance—which in those days referred to European nations, not to British trade unions—Mesopotamia, Little Englanders, women's suffrage, tariff reform, passive resistance (I suppose Mr Gandhi had started getting himself arrested), Sarajevo, mobilization.

All these words and phrases became part of a shorthand/longhand vocabulary of no interest to other boys of twelve or thirteen, certainly not to those known to me; and they were of interest to me largely as a form of retaliation against my brother Harold's flaunted logarithms, cosines and tangents, meaningless words (now as then) because mathematics has always been a closed book to me. But in retrospect, though I find it difficult to understand how any school curriculum could have excluded all opportunity for explaining these matters to the children of the time, I am certain that at school they were barely mentioned. School had to be boring, and no one tried to relieve the boredom. There had lately been 'strikes' at elementary schools in various parts of the country, the scholars demanding an extra half-holiday a week and the abolition of caning. A *Daily Graphic* cartoonist depicted a swarm of low-browed urchins holding aloft home-made banners saying DOWN WITH SKOOL. The strikes were not successful, and I remember no attempt to introduce an overtime ban, a go-slow, or a work-to-rule. Perhaps the last-named might have proved too painful, since it could have involved learning something.

It follows that the ideas and views I picked up and unconsciously adopted as my own were mostly those of the egregious Horatio Bottomley, the founder (in 1906) and editor of the strident and enormously successful scandal-mongering weekly *John Bull*. I have no idea how many passages of his tub-thumping and platitudinous prose I struggled to put into shorthand at my mother's deadpan dictation, but my father held him in high esteem and read him with weekly approval—and so did Grandma Hewitt. I didn't then know that Bottomley had been an orphanage child (he claimed, falsely I believe, that he was the son of Charles Bradlaugh); but I did know that, from being an errand boy, he had taught himself Pitman's and become a court shorthand-writer. However, notwithstanding this admirable beginning, Bottomley later became my archetype of the silver-tongued swindler, the predator with the gift-of-the-gab. I don't think I then knew much about the suspected criminality and the bankruptcy that had led to his resignation from Parliament in 1912, and at the time he was a popular idol likely to survive almost anything. But my parents must have known, for as early as 1908 Bottomley had appeared at the Old Bailey (and my father was on duty there at the time) on charges of conspiracy to defraud and, as he was to do many times, had talked a jury into acquitting him. Having launched *John Bull*, which swept him into public favour and which gained a three-million circulation during the Kaiser's War, he was paid by the Government to make patriotic recruiting speeches all over the country; and it wasn't until he was again an MP in 1922, by which time I myself was in the police service, that he was at last convicted of fraud and sentenced to seven years' penal servitude, a multi-millionaire made deservedly penniless. My father's lifelong confidence in such a man was a shock to me, even though it did not distinguish my father from millions of other Englishmen. I had even won an essay prize at school, the only school prize I ever won for anything, by concluding a fanfare of patriotism with *John Bull*'s weekly front page motto from Act Five of *King John*, not because it was *King John* but because it was *John Bull*:

> Come the three corners of the world in arms
> And we shall shock them; nought shall make us rue
> If England to itself do rest but true.

England to itself rested true enough to sustain, adulate, and applaud that incredible hypocrite throughout my childhood and adolescence; and his exposure pulled the rug from under two whole generations of my elders and betters.

I hope I have not presented myself as a studious, bookish, and clever boy, happier to be learning and acquiring skills than to be playing in the street. I was to be weaned from playing in the street only when it was pitch dark out there; studious only in the winter. And in the winter I could support only three kinds of study—English, French, and shorthand. My homework in those three subjects was always done before tea-time and available to any schoolmate who cared to call round and lend me his arithmetic, algebra, geometry, physics, chemistry, or geography homework for totally uncomprehending transcription. But at about that time, for the light evenings, there appeared a new variety of street pastimes.

Warlike weapons had been appearing in the toy-shop windows and, in due course, in the streets. The Sidney Street Siege of 1911 had aroused interest in that deadly and haphazard little firework, the Mauser automatic pistol. Indeed it was said at the time that Mr Winston Churchill, then Home Secretary, wanted the police to have Mausers and was dissuaded only by being encouraged to try one himself. Imitation Mausers appeared as 'spring guns' with a tiny spring-operated plunger for ejecting small marbles, ball-bearings or pebbles, and they appeared too as pocket torches and water-pistols. In 1913 a water-pistol was used for squirting ammonia into the face of a night-watchman at a Newgate Street bank; and as the toy manufacturers began producing imitation Webley-Scott revolvers (firing coils of percussion caps like a modern automatic weapon) these were taken into use by criminals as a method of intimidation—and not prohibited until 1938.

Even the peashooter, which I hadn't seen anywhere since my Finsbury Park days, appeared in the shops to use up good pocket-money. But you could make a perfectly good pea-shooter from a length of the $\frac{3}{8}$-inch brass tubing sold as curtain-rod, fitting it with a more or less hygienic mouthpiece made from a large cork. Suddenly in 1912–13 the peashooter was everywhere, it seemed, as an instrument of aggression; though of course the essence of peashooting is that the victim or target is unaware, non-provocative, and unable to see his assailant. Peashooting, that is to say, is a furtive sport, not a means of battle.

There also came into use at about this time a kind of toy bomb, comprising a quartered ball of lead about the size of an acorn, which hung from the fingers on the end of a string. When you slackened the string the four segments fell slightly apart and you could insert percussion caps in the apertures. A pull on the string then tightened it all up. You whirled it round and let it go straight up into the air. Its arrival on the ground produced a satisfying bang. There seemed to be a great and growing need for bigger bangs. A halfpenny would buy four 'slap-bangs', little screws of thin red paper containing gun-powder and gravel, which you could toss out of hedge-fronted gardens behind passing walkers, though for a satisfying bang these really needed to be lobbed into the open window of an echoing bathroom in which someone was singing. Slap-bangs were also known in my circle as flapper-scarers, which I take to signify that we were become aware of girls as sex-objects and were approaching the barmy stage of adolescence.

But there was only one way of producing a really big bang, and it is a method that seems now to have been mercifully forgotten. I think this is odd, because its practitioners were the original 'latch-key kids', children with working mums entrusted with the front-door key to let themselves into a lonely house when they got home from school. It needed the kind of key with a hollow barrel. One end of a four-foot string was tied to the key-handle and the other end to the wards, so that the key could be hung from the hands horizontally. Then the barrel of the key was stuffed with the sulphur and phosphorus from the heads of half a dozen 'strike anywhere' matches; and these were gently rammed down with a long wire nail which came to rest with its head protruding an inch from the end of the key-barrel. Holding the string with both hands so that the key was horizontal, you bashed the head of the nail against a wall. Sometimes the bang was truly astonishing, audible streets away. Sometimes, too, the whole key split open and had to be written off, but more often the explosion merely blew the nail out like a bullet, to hit the wall again and fall to the ground.

It was at about this time also that there developed a strange craze for old pram-wheels, not just for use on steerable go-carts but as mono-wheels propelled and guided with a stick. A short piece of dowel rod was driven through the axle-hole, so as to protrude nine inches on one side and three on the other, giving the wheel a bias. This rod was greased so that the pro-pelling stick, held against it, would drive the wheel smoothly forward, rolling at a slight angle from the perpendicular. Some-times in cornering to the left, the wheel would begin to slant too much and needed a swift tap under the three-inch side of the axle. Some boys developed an astonishing skill with this simple contraption, and teams of them could perform inter-weaving exercises in the middle of the road which, on a music-hall stage, would almost have merited a roll of drums. It was even more satisfying than the iron hoop, it called for strange and unique little skills, and I do not know why it has died out.

But die out it did, like many other street games, with the imminence of war that was clouding the early part of 1914; especially the bang-producing pastimes, which began to be for-bidden by nervous parents. Another street nuisance which appeared in Fulham at that time had a very brief life and may well have owed its early death to the general state of tension. This was the window-tapper, suitable only for sash-windows because it used the overhang of the upper half-window. It also needed a windy evening. With chewing gum or cobbler's wax we secured one end of an 18-inch length of black cotton to the centre of one of the glass panels in the upper half of the window. At the other end, about nine inches below the window-frame centre and two inches from the glass of the lower window, hung a half-inch metal nut or a pebble with a hole in it; and just above the nut or pebble would be fixed four stiff-paper wings to catch the wind. A decent breeze would have the thing tapping irregularly at the window, and as a rule the occupier would come out a surprising number of times before he decided to investigate and then found our evilly-inspired apparatus. This of course was a spectator sport, and a group of us would be watching from somewhere across the road.

But the percussion cap pistols came out again, old walking sticks were converted into dummy rifles, and the Prussophobia of the past ten years became so universal among my street-urchin comrades that no one along the whole road wanted to be a German and it was difficult to arrange battles. David Blüm-berg, my little Jewish protégé (or thus I now liked to see him) had never made any secret of his father's German nationality; and although in the ordinary way he would not have been victimized—he was a gentle, eager, sweet-natured boy with huge dark eyes and a heavily-freckled face—his difference from the rest of us was already made prominent by his absence from the classroom during Scripture lessons in the morning. David was the first victim known to me of the crackpot anti-Germanism of the next few years; of, indeed, the rest of my life.

I knew about the assassination at Sarajevo on 28 June, I knew that the shots were fired by a Serbian student (I even knew his name), I knew that the dead man was called Archduke Franz Ferdinand of Austria-Hungary and that he was soon to be an Emperor of somewhere. I've often wished I could read a German history of those days, for the newspaper articles and the *John Bull* rhetoric I was regularly committing to Pitman's shorthand at the back-parlour table made it seem that the Kaiser and the Austrian Emperor were sub-human monsters intent on either dominating or destroying Europe, while Britain was blessed with far-sighted statesmen who could see the horrors that would attend any great war in the twentieth cen-tury and were determined to find 'peaceful solutions'. But the idea of a solution suggested that there must be a problem, and I could never understand what problems they were trying to find peaceful solutions to. If the problem was really one of 'naked aggression' (I can see the Pitman's outline for that now), I didn't see how that could be peacefully solved. And I didn't know anyone to ask.

One morning during those pre-war months David Blümberg came back to his desk after Scripture and sat on a seat which someone, in his absence, had smeared with fish-glue. The teacher told him sharply to stop squirming about, and it was an hour or more before his plight was discovered—I suppose by then it was playtime. As he stood up his shorts were torn, the skin had peeled off his bare legs, and he was in tears. I don't remember that there was much enquiry about this, but a flattened and empty fish-glue tube was discovered on the classroom floor. Neither can I recall whether it was before or after the outbreak of war that we started calling the Germans 'Huns', but some classroom wit had soon rechristened David Blümberg 'Hunberg' and it became a nickname of hate. A little later he was universally known as von Zeppelin. It was David's lot to be in the right place at the right time for a persecution which even the mildest of the boys were ready to tolerate, and I felt I had never seen anything so degrading or so productive of vicarious and helpless anger. His school satchel was thrown over a high wall into a factory yard, his school cap was filled with horse-dung, he was shouted and sneered at, his parents and his country were abused. And I wish I could remember that I stood up for him at the time, or ranged myself at his side to share the torment. To my shame, I recall nothing of the sort.

On the morning of 5 August 1914 my father, who had returned from the City very late the previous night, had a story to tell. He was at this time in charge, as Acting Chief Inspector, of one of the four police divisions in the City; deputizing, in fact, for a senior officer absent on prolonged sick leave. These duties had greatly diminished the time he could spend with us at home, and from this historic date they were going to diminish it still further. His rank at that time was called District Inspector, and I take this opportunity to say that, among all the police officers I have known, of whatever rank, he came the closest to my ideal in appearance, personality, rectitude and conscientiousness. He still does. 'I suppose,' he used to say, 'I was cut out for public service of some kind, and I don't quite know what else I might have done.' I don't know what else he would have done with such distinction, and I came to know that he was regarded 'in the City' with the same respect that he earned from us at home. On this eventful morning he told us that the previous night Hammersmith Broadway had been crammed with people waiting to learn what 'the German reply' was. Britain had told the German Government to withdraw its troops from Belgium, invaded two days before as part of the Schlieffen Plan in German war strategy. If no favourable reply was received by midnight, Britain and Germany would be at war. My father had come out of the Metropolitan Underground railway station to get on a Fulham Palace Road tram, and found that all road traffic was immobilized by the crowds. As he was resignedly walking home he heard behind him their 'sudden mad roar' of excitement and belligerence as the news spread among them that we were at war with Germany. Yet he was home, mother said, by 11.30 p.m. Was the news premature? I had never understood about the alleged 'midnight' deadline until I read in Mr A. J. P. Taylor's *English History 1914-1945*:

At 10.30 p.m. on 4 August 1914 the King held a privy council at Buckingham Place. . . . This council sanctioned the proclamation of a state of war with Germany from 11 p.m. Why 11 p.m.? It is impossible to say. The ultimatum to Germany demanded an answer *here* (i.e. London) by midnight. After its dispatch someone unknown recollected that German time was an hour in advance of Greenwich mean time, and it was decided that the ultimatum should expire according to the time in Berlin. Why? Perhaps for fear that the German government might give a favourable, or equivocal, answer; perhaps to get things settled and to be able to go to bed; probably for no reason at all.

But apart from the shocking outbreak of anti-German violence, the most vivid of my early recollections of the Kaiser's

War concerned my beloved playground, Bishop's Park. One such memory is the sound, audible from my bedroom, of bugles calling Reveille, Cookhouse, Last Post, etc. to the troops hurriedly encamped there; it used to move my father's ears like those of an old war-horse. Another was a pierrot concert party in the bandstand singing Ivor Novello's 'Keep the Home Fires Burning', which I have always thought one of the simplest, neatest and most unforgettable melodies ever written.

I knew boys who gleefully took part in the mad and cruel attacks on German shops and houses. David Blümberg's house in Lambrook Terrace had all its front windows smashed, and someone told me that all the little leaded panes in the front door had been broken individually as if with a hammer. Our favourite baker's shop in Munster Road, whose name was Geib (everyone called it Geebs), not merely had its windows smashed but all the bread and cakes were taken from the display window and then there was an attempt to set the place alight. Mr. Geib's principal claim to my affection was that he had always supplied, as 'makeweight', the most delicious little loaves (they were like 'tin loaves' for dolls) which you could eat new in a couple of ecstatic mouthfuls. 'Makeweight' was the means by which bakers complied with the law about the weight of the 'standard loaf', which was prescribed by Parliament but could not always be satisfied in the days of simpler bakery.

My brother Harold was chased home from a Fulham Palace Road bus-stop by an angry mob because he had tried, on his way home from school, to stop some children throwing lighted matches into the open basement windows of a German hair-dresser's shop. Any firm with a name that was not obviously British was in danger from the mob. Long-cherished names like Gluckstein were painted out and succeeded by impersonal ones like The Premier Stores. Even Camerer Cuss & Co., those long-established dealers in antique and modern clocks and watches (still flourishing, I'm happy to say, in New Oxford Street), found it necessary to put the following advertisement in the *West London Observer* on 14 August. It was so quaintly un-English as to recall the proverb *qui s'excuse s'accuse*:

A DISCLAIMER. Camerer Cuss & Co., whose business has been established in London for 120 years, the proprietors of which are BRITISH SUBJECTS, emphatically deny the false and baseless rumours that their establishment in Uxbridge Road has been raided by the police, and will give a substantial reward to any person giving such information as will lead to the conviction of anyone now circulating such falsehoods. We are loyal BRITISH SUBJECTS and most heartily say GOD SAVE THE KING and the British Empire.

I didn't know anyone who had heard such a rumour; but I am in no doubt that we all believed the spreading of such stories was in some way criminal (which it wasn't). And by way of analogy my father recalled to us a story about the captured Chinese 'rebels', during the Boxer Rebellion of 1900, who in surrendering used to throw up their hands with the ingratiating assertion 'Kleen Victolia belly good man'. But there was nothing funny about the plight of firms like Camerer Cuss & Co., and if their patriotic 'Disclaimer' looked idiotic, it was after all addressed to idiots.

What was it all about? My brothers and I understood that the war had come because someone had killed the Archduke Ferdinand. If this was an inadequate reason for Armageddon, I can't remember that it seemed so at the time. History lessons had always taught us about the War of Jenkins' Ear, the War of This and That, none of them seeming to justify the mass murder they all led to. But we must have been typical of millions in our excited and rather bewildered surprise that war was not, after all, confined to the history books; and in a rather dumb sort of way I supposed that this explained the hysterical cheering my father had told us about. I knew that people were going to be killed and that this would supply the atmosphere in which you could have heroes and Victoria Crosses.

But being at war seemed to make little difference, at first. It was on my 13th birthday, Sunday 23 August 1914, that the Belgians in Mons went to church in the morning unaware that one of the significant battles of history was about to engulf them. Even so, it seems now to have been an indecisive skirmish followed by a long and ghastly British retreat. In the newspapers during that week, however, there was nothing about any British retreat. Instead there were stories of German atrocities that were utterly bewildering to read about. Belgian babies were being tossed on bayonets like bags of grain, Belgian women were being raped, mutilated and then shot, villagers were being herded into their churches and village halls, locked in and burned to death. What had all this to do with battle, fighting and heroism, the Charge of the Light Brigade, and How Horatius Kept the Bridge? Nothing, said my father, there were always these terrible stories at the start of any war. But were they true, we wanted to know, could they be true? He didn't know.

I asked David Blümberg, and on my behalf he asked his German father. Mr. Blümberg, he said, told him they were not true and that they were made up by the Germans themselves, to strike terror into civilian populations and then spread it abroad by way of the refugees. Within a week, as if in support of this explanation, there had arrived 400,000 Belgian refugees, bringing their own stories of the atrocities. I do not remember whether they had witnessed the deeds they described or had been told about them, but I suspect the latter.

The plight of the Belgians and the growing hostility of their reception, at least in Fulham, began to upset Harold and therefore myself. Once you are aware of a new and foreign element in the community, it seems to be ubiquitous. Belgian children were in our schools, in our houses (though there were none in mine), in our games, everywhere. I found it exciting that there could actually be boys and girls who knew no other language than French, that what I had learned at school was not a classroom invention, and (above all) that these children actually spoke the kind of Franglais that was always crossed through in my homework books. Example: a Belgian boy we all knew as René wanted to know Roland's name. And he did *not* say 'Comment s'appelle-t-il?' He said, as I would have said in my ignorance, 'Quel est son nom?' Listening to the Belgian children's French was very subversive.

Someone told us they were all 'working-class' children,

speaking their own language badly. But I thought this all a part of the custom, which grew quite rapidly, of denigrating them as lazy, dirty, avaricious, and immoral, the very labels we keep handy today for immigrants of the wrong tint. It was said that they had all arrived in a state of resentment and confusion at being driven from their homes, that they thought the British and the French had neglected the defence of their country's neutrality. It was said above all that they would compete with the British in the labour market; which was odd, since the British labour market seemed to need workers of every conceivable kind to replace the millions of young men being taken away for the armed forces. These things went unexplained.

My mother announced in the first few days of the war that our contribution to victory was going to be the permanent (as distinct from the hitherto occasional) substitution of margarine for butter. None of us minded much, but it led to a fierce argument as to how we were going to pronounce it. 'Marjerene' had the respectable authority, for my father and me, of *Pitman's Shorthand Dictionary*. Harold's scorn was unbounded. The word, he said (he had been looking it up), came from margaric acid, which was the fatty stuff in all sorts of animal and vegetable oils. It was margarine with a hard g. Unfortunately for my father his revered *Nuttall's Standard Dictionary of the English Language, Based on the Labours of the Most Eminent Lexicographers*, said 'mahr-gar-een (occasionally, and erroneously, mahr-ja-reen)'. He was terribly torn, but in the end he lined up with the hard g, while the rest of us varied according to the company we found ourselves in (it was a soft g, anyway, in the shops). And it wasn't until 1916 that E. V. Knox disarmed everyone by declaring in *Punch*: 'I take thee, dearest margarine, for butter or for worse.'

Employed by the friendly blacksmith Mr Yellowlees in Dawes Road was a very young man named Baynard, whom the boys of the district hardly knew because he was taciturn and, we thought, disapproved of his employer's generosity in the matter of repairing iron hoops without charge. It turned out, to everyone's surprise, that Baynard was a regular Army reservist;

and when he was 'recalled to the colours' in the first week of August his prestige among the boys went through the roof. I can recall feeling greatly impressed, too, that the authorities should know with such speed and certainty where all the reservists lived, and the impression was that of an awakening lion gathering itself for the spring. But Mr Baynard was caught in the retreat from Mons, he had a bullet wound in the neck, and he must have been almost the first British soldier in the whole war to be back in civvies with a wound stripe on his sleeve—he was certainly back before the middle of September 1914. He wore the wound stripe on his sleeve as a protection against the young women who went around handing white feathers to any men of seeming military age who were not in uniform.

It was while we were still on holiday from school, and there-fore must have been in the first week of September, that Mr Baynard was seen by some of the boys back at the Dawes Road smithy (I was not among them) and was induced to tell his story of the retreat. We British seem to have a way of cherishing our defeats as if they were victories of some special kind, and indeed I suppose Mons and Dunkirk both merit the back-handed tribute that, if they 'snatched defeat from the jaws of victory', they also supplied—at fabulous cost—important lessons both in tactics and in strategy, extracting huge armies from the kind of débâcle that has usually ended in total surren-der. Years later I came to know a number of men who had survived the retreat from Mons; and they all said that if it had come near the end of a war instead of the very beginning, it would certainly have been a surrender. Mr Baynard, of the Royal Horse Artillery, had been tottering on foot with thou-sands of other men through Le Cateau to Soissons, a thirteen-day nightmare of marching with inadequate food and seldom more than three hours sleep in a night; and he told of men literally marching in their sleep, held up by others. On the sixth day, he said, they had been passing a heap of discarded Cycling Corps bicycles. Watching other men grabbing them and riding off, he bitterly regretted that he had never learned to ride. And then he suddenly selected one that looked sound, got on and rode it—zigzagging for some miles—all the way to Soissons. He was our local hero, and I think it made absolutely no difference that his story happened to be one of defeat and running away. We were all proud and glad to see him alive and back at the smithy. Mr Baynard's war was over.

Arthur Wheeler's was just beginning. In mid-August he had enlisted in the Seventh (City of London) Regiment—the 'Shiny Seventh'. Arthur was my stepmother's adopted son, about fifteen years my senior and a signalman on the Central London Railway. It is through him that my memory carries an imperishable association between 'Alexander's Ragtime Band', then being sung and whistled everywhere, and the wearing of puttees. This may be partly because both seem to me perfect examples of an idea that should have been decently smothered, the Irving Berlin melody because of its clumsiness and its absurd lyric, and puttees because they are inefficient, unhygienic, and time-wasting. But it is mainly because Arthur Wheeler, unwinding his ten yards of puttees before our parlour fire (he took them off at every opportunity because they were 'bad for me legs'), used to hum or whistle 'Alexander's Ragtime Band' as he did so, tapping his foot the while. My father, who had seen puttees in use in India, thought they were 'an utter absurdity'; but Arthur used to say that when you had to pack them instead of wearing them they took up less room than leggings did, and that in emergencies they could be used as slings and bandages. As an infantryman, he had to begin winding his at the ankle and tie them at the knee; while Mr Baynard, as a cavalryman, had had to begin at the knee and tie at the ankle, because the rubbing of the wearer's knee against the horse's flank would otherwise undo the tape. The British brought the idea from India, where the *putti* is still worn by multitudes; and at the time the British seemed to infect every other European army with it except the German, who stuck to leggings and jackboots.

It was after the summer holiday of 1914 that I graduated to long trousers (or 'long-'uns') and was able to feel more at one with the boys in *The Magnet* and *The Gem* illustrations. Harold had been wearing long-'uns for years, retaining an impressive crease down the front of each leg by putting them under his mattress at night. But despite those illustrations, he and his little clique at school thought long-'uns looked absurd with a school cap, and accordingly kept their caps in their satchels, for use only in emergencies. Needless to say I thought the same, but never wore a school cap anyway. One consequence of this was that, once in long-'uns, I began to receive white feathers in the street from vicariously patriotic young women. I was large for my age and probably looked seventeen or eighteen, but made a practice of accepting the white feather before saying 'I'm only fourteen', and I think I must have been rather proud of being thought soldier-like. The mood of the time was neatly captured in an asinine Paul Rubens song:

> We don't want to lose you
> But we think you ought to go.
> Your King and your country
> Both need you so.

And this was to go on for another eighteen months before the Government, in response to a newspaper clamour, introduced a scheme of compulsory military service. The position seems to have been, whatever the newspapers were saying and the ladies with the white feathers implying, that the Army already had far more men than it could train and equip. It would need no more men until about the end of 1916. But there were fiercely patriotic politicians who were determined to get conscription introduced as a political gesture, and there were Ministers threatening to resign if the Government refused. The story was put about that there were a million 'slackers' in the community who would never volunteer and would have to be fetched. To the worried Mr Asquith, still Prime Minister, there then came the devious idea of getting men of military age to 'attest' that they would be willing to serve if called upon. Lord Derby was given the job of organizing this scheme, and men who had 'attested' under it were given a khaki arm-band to wear in public as a defence against the white-feather movement.

The Lord Derby scheme gave rise to the famous phrase, 'Quick, I want three volunteers, you, you and you'. It paved the way, as it was meant to do, for the Military Service Act of 1916 which came into force on 9 February.

It was towards the end of 1914 that I made the acquaintance of Miss Lillian Herbert, daughter of my much-loved Mr Herbert of the Sunday School. To me she seemed middle-aged, but was I suppose thirty to thirty-five, a quiet and gentle creature who walked with a crutch because of some deformity. At this time she lived with her father in a large house in Stevenage Road, a rather posh thoroughfare which ran alongside the Bishop's Park; and whereas it might have been supposed that, in the usual sense, she looked after him, my impression was rather that he looked after her. Her importance in this story is that she gave piano lessons, usually to pupils who went to her house. I discovered that she was a pianist on one memorable summer's evening when, through the Herberts' open front window, I heard her playing Christian Sinding's *Rustle of Spring*—which, at that time, everyone seemed to be playing or aspiring to play. (My father said the composer was far more sinned against than Sinding.) Thereafter I made it a practice, at the end of any of Mr Herbert's organized 'excursions' for the Sunday School mob, to walk with him to the gate of his house in the hope of finding Miss Lillian at home and getting her to play request items. I don't think I realized what an imposition this kind of thing can be.

But I soon discovered the bond between the Herberts' household and ours: we both possessed two fat volumes known as the *Star Folios*, a Paxton publication (long, alas, out of print) in which all the standard overtures and many shorter orchestral compositions had been skilfully arranged for solo piano. My father had acquired these for flute practice, but I had always longed to hear some good pianist play them. The names at the page-tops were truly exciting—*Masaniello, Crown Diamonds, Fra Diavolo, Poet and Peasant, Rosamunde, L'Italiana in Algieri, The Caliph of Baghdad, La Gazza Ladra, The Barber of Seville, The Magic Flute, Oberon.* Miss Lillian could play them all, with (I suppose) mechanical accuracy—I cannot describe the

excitement of watching and hearing one pair of hands producing those marvellous sequences of sound, and I take it to be
some sort of comment on my own musical taste that I should
have found it so deeply satisfying. Years later, of course, I
considered myself in good company when I discovered (on
gramophone records) the Liszt piano transcriptions from Verdi
operas; but these were too showy for me, too much Liszt and
not enough Verdi. Those *Star Folios* must be collectors' pieces
today.

At about this time there occurred two memorable episodes
at school. Both involved me in trouble, the first deservedly and
the second, I think, not. The first concerned the jumping
walnut, a device which I have neither seen nor heard of (I
wonder why?) since about 1914. To make a jumping walnut
you took half a walnut shell and bored little holes (ideally with
a red-hot needle, more clumsily with a fretwork drill) on each
side of it near the rim—roughly where the gunwales would be if
it were a dinghy. Through these holes you passed a length of
cobbler's thread, tying it so as to make a tight loop. With a
one-inch wire nail you twisted the loop round and round like
a tourniquet, until you judged that the tension was only just
below breaking-point for the sides of the shell. Then you
pressed the end of the nail into a piece of warmed cobbler's
wax (or, less satisfactorily, a cud of chewing gum) stuck to
the narrower end of the shell, stood the contraption upside
down on the ground and waited. As the nail slowly disengaged
itself from the wax, the strain among the spectators was only
just endurable. Suddenly the walnut shell leaped high into
the air, with a crack as the head of the nail sprang round. It was
a deeply satisfying contrivance, since the tension of the waiting
period could he heightened by planting this little time-bomb
near some unsuspecting victim. I remember that I once steal-
thily put one on the floor under the hem of Grandma Hewitt's
skirt, and that its upward leap was not well received.

The one that got me into more serious trouble was placed
on a teacher's desk at school, hidden under a sheet of notepaper. Although it nearly hit the ceiling and was caught on the

way down by a boy named Denbigh (who normally couldn't catch anything), the startled master saw only the fluttering sheet of notepaper and was at a loss to know what had happened. Then the harassed man concluded that he had been shot at with a catapult, and angrily demanded that the weapon be surrendered. After that it was no longer possible not to laugh, and the unanimous guffaw made him far angrier. He announced that the whole class would stay there, after school hours, until the catapultist had come forward. And when school hours were over it became apparent that he meant what he said. As I was the owner of the jumping walnut it seemed that I had no alternative but to stand up and admit it, which I did without heroism because everyone knew it was mine. The class was detained just long enough to see me caned; and afterwards, as I pressed my throbbing hands into my armpits, I glumly reflected that there were some teachers who would have taken it all as a joke, and probably some who would have asked for instruction in the manufacture of jumping walnuts.

The other episode embroiled my mother, of all people, with my form master. It was the only time in my life when I was sent home for having dirty boots, or dirty anything. In the playground before school began in the morning, everyone ran or lolled about until one of the teachers rang a handbell. Then we all had to form up into classes, on marks that were allotted to us for the term, and there ensued a kind of kit inspection. One morning the master inspecting me observed that my boots were dusty, as indeed they were for I had been playing on a roadside sand-heap; and he ordained that I was to go home at once and clean them. When I got home at about 9.15 and reported to my incredulous mother that I had been sent home to clean my boots, she almost exploded with indignation. She made me brush the sand off my boots but then insisted, to my dumb horror, on coming back to school with me to confront this unique martinet who seemed to suppose that parents should follow and superintend their offspring until the last moment before the handbell was rung. What passed between them I never knew, but she told me afterwards that he had apologized.

I remember thinking, with my usual perversity, that it was a bit hard for a man to have to apologize for doing what I supposed, after all, must be his job.

*

The German Zeppelin had hovered over our lives since I was a baby, for the first of its kind had been successfully flown in the year of my birth. It had always been interesting: the war suddenly made it frightening. Germany was ahead of all other countries in the development of airships that were steerable (for some reason this was always called 'dirigible'), and Count von Zeppelin's design has never, apparently, been surpassed. It seemed to me that the Zeppelin was always in the news, and since the word news is synonymous with bad tidings we had heard only about Zeppelin disasters.

But in the autumn of 1914 everyone seemed to expect devastating Zeppelin raids on London and the principal cities. One evening in October as I was getting into bed we heard distant anti-aircraft guns firing at something—or it may have been at nothing, we never learned what had happened. I remember only that they sounded like distant drums, and that I was ashamed to discover that I was thoroughly frightened, the fear being greatly increased by the fact that I was standing in my extremely short under-vest and struggling in the dark to find the way into my flannelette nightshirt. My brothers and I had never had a light to go to bed with, not even a candle—any naked light, my father thought, would be far too dangerous. The bedroom door stood permanently open, normally admitting a little vague light from downstairs, though the gas lamp in the hall was never lighted unless we had visitors. Once the war began, even that came to an end. The Defence of the Realm Act and its subordinate legislation controlled how much light we were to display, and in our house this seemed to amount to a Stygian blackness. Incidentally we had no heating in any bedroom: there was a fireplace in which a fire might be made if you were ill and the doctor recommended it—an excitement such as would make any kind of illness worth while. But normally we went to bed in the dark and with no heating, even in the coldest winters. The odd thing is that I have absolutely no recollection of ever feeling cold in the bedroom, or indeed anywhere. Under similar treatment, I feel, my own children would all have died and I should have repeatedly appeared at the Old Bailey on charges of manslaughter by negligence.

Similarly, in the mornings we washed in cold water in the bathroom. This was a genuine bathroom, in the sense that it was a room with a bath in it, to which warm water occasionally found its way when (as sometimes happened) the kitchen range had been so adjusted as to send it there. But it had no hand-basin. Instead there was a high wooden splay-legged table like a huge saw-bench, unpainted and deeply scored with the wrinkles of the years, on which stood a tin bowl and a bar of red carbolic soap, often disguised under the name of Nubolic. We filled the tin bowl by holding it under the bath-tap, and it says much for our unquenchable optimism that we always held it first under the tap marked H, though rarely with any distinguishable result. I do not pretend that we had any kind of a Spartan childhood, but in these matters it was fairly primitive.

I thought the first Zeppelin raid came shortly before that Christmas of 1914, but the records show that it was on 14 April 1915 at Tyneside, and that there was no loss of life and little damage. They also show that the very next day there were Zeppelin bombs on Lowestoft, Southwold, Faversham, and Sittingbourne—whose total effect was that at Sittingbourne one blackbird was killed. I thought this was the kind of story that could never survive the war and the resumption of something like accuracy in the news. But I was wrong: the story keeps on cropping up in histories of the Kaiser's War. All through April and May the Zeppelins were bombing East Anglian and Kentish towns, and then on 14 May 1915 ninety bombs were dropped on London and ten people killed. Those bombs, wherever they were, could be clearly heard in Fulham. They rattled the windows. Roland and I were in bed and my mother came to tell us there was a 'gas warning'—which of course would have sounded much more alarming during Hitler's

War but at that time merely meant that the gas company had tipped off its customers that an air raid was imminent by dimming all their gas lamps three times in quick succession. Roland, then about nine years old, was unwilling to wake up and I called to him as I pulled my trousers on. 'What's up?' he said sleepily. 'Zeppelins,' I said excitedly (I was very frightened); 'come on, get dressed.' And so *he* was frightened. We all sat in the back parlour, no one knowing what we should do if a Zeppelin bomb fell on the house. No bomb, so far as I know, ever fell within miles of the house.

My father of course was not at home. At that time he was either in the City already or had left home as soon as the gas warning came. But my mother had not yet gone to bed, and her demeanour was superb and in the best sense exemplary. I think it may have been a Sunday evening, for she was wearing the brown lace blouse and the very high lace collar (with whalebone stiffeners) with which, once the midday meal was over and the washing-up done, she always honoured the Sabbath. She said we were not to be frightened, that we could soon go back to bed, and that she would get us some cocoa. She was very controlled, except that she spilled cocoa in every saucer.

And it was at about this time that there built up at home the expectation that, sooner or later, my father would be officially promoted to Chief Inspector, the police rank in which he had been 'acting' for many months owing to the illness of someone higher up, and that we should all have to move to the City. I don't know about my two brothers, but I was able to stoke up considerable prestige, both at school and in the street, on account of this imminent move into *the* danger area. But in fact it remained imminent for so long that the prestige began to wear a bit thin; and I realize now how little we all knew about the process by which an 'imminent' police promotion, or I suppose any public service promotion, is conferred after all upon someone else. However, in January 1916 it happened at last. My father told us all one evening of his promotion. And Annie Palmer, the poor stone-deaf maid-of-all-work who had been with us since I was a baby, knew from all our faces what it was that my father was saying. She abruptly left the room and was later found in the kitchen, crying; for she had known throughout the long 'imminence' of the promotion that when we moved to the City she would have to find other accommodation.

This sad little episode reminds me that, because of my father's heavy and growing involvement in the war-time policing of the City, we were seeing very little of him at that time. He was often unable to get home at night because of air raids or other war emergencies, and to us he began to seem like someone absent on active service. It also suggests to my memory that, accordingly, he was rather more ruthless about poor Annie and her future than was characteristic of him.

Another consequence of his detachment was that some other member of the family (and we took it in turns) had to tend his considerable congregation of cage-birds. He had about thirty-five in cages of various shapes and sizes, the main cage being very large, barely portable, shaped like the Crystal Palace, and filled with thirty canaries. They were nearly all the progeny of an original couple called Dick and Betty, and I think he kept them all because he couldn't bear to part with them. Other cages contained linnets and goldfinches, and always at breeding times there were one or two sitting birds peering coldly and one-sidedly at us from the rims of their little nesting-basins. Some of these birds were members of the family, and were allowed out in the evenings to fly about the parlour, perching wherever they liked until it was time for them to be caught with a duster and returned to their cages. My father was curiously sentimental and sentimentally curious about all these birds; and once when a hen canary hatched out three babies who died almost at once he reported with solemn emotion that there were tears in her eyes. Nothing would ever shake his certainty about this crying canary, and over the years we heard him telling countless strangers and visitors about it until we nearly cried ourselves. I think most of us got even closer to crying when someone left open the door of the 'Crystal Palace' cage while it was out on the balcony of the Gowan

Avenue house, and more than thirty escaped canaries perched themselves in the trees along the road. Very few of them were recaptured. My father was deeply dejected about this, his dejection taking the form of a total inability to talk about it.

I should like to say a little more about Annie, for with hindsight I believe that the true reason why she could not come with us to the City, to live in official quarters where she would be much observed, was that my father thought her such an oddity. And an oddity she was. But if there was room for her at Gowan Avenue there certainly was in the City, where we had twice the accommodation. He had 'given her a home' some fifteen years before, when she came to our door at 101 Wood-stock Road, Finsbury Park, seeking food and shelter for the night, and was allowed to stay indefinitely as a kind of unpaid home help because her only possible alternative was the work-house. I think she must have been already known to my parents, possibly from a time when, as teenagers, they had all attended the Flood Street Mission in Chelsea. Certainly my mother told us that Annie had lost her hearing because, having as a child particularly beautiful hair which her proud mother was con-stantly washing, she was always being sent to school with wet hair over her ears. I never heard of a less likely cause of deafness, but we all accepted it; and certainly, whatever the cause, Annie was now totally deaf, there was absolutely no residual hearing that could have been helped by any mechanical or other means. My father taught himself the deaf-and-dumb alphabet, in the hope that she would let him teach her and draw her a little more into the family circle—in every other way she lived as one of the family. But she would have none of it. She preferred to lip-read—though she usually had to be told things in scribbled notes—and to use her own strange, squeaky voice which was sometimes so difficult to understand. Her corn-coloured hair was always plentiful, but always bunched up in the mountainous sugar-loaf fashion of the times. But she had a perpetually shiny, slightly imbecile face and protruding eyes; and even as a young woman she seemed to walk with an aged shuffle, wearing shapeless clothes and never seeming to want any others.

Her main interest in life was my brother Roland, who was born after she joined the household and in relation to whom she displayed a possessiveness that could become almost ferocious. She had had much to do with his care and upbringing, and I truly believe she would have given her life for him. I think of her with nothing but sadness, fed by remorse that I should have treated her (I believe) so badly. Shortly before we moved, a room was found for her in Fulham, whence she came to the City on Mondays to do the week's washing, until my father retired in 1922 and went to live elsewhere.

My father would not allow her to go out after dark, for then, he said, she would be deprived of two senses, sight as well as hearing, and she would have no means of recognizing danger. Occasionally on a winter's evening my mother would relax this rule sufficiently for her to go along to Jackson's, the dairy in Munster Road, to get margarine, cheese, or sugar. But when the street lamps were dimmed during the war, this too came to an end and it fell to my lot, or Harold's, to do any such emergency shopping. I was reminded of this by the following item I found in the Minutes of the Fulham Borough Council for 28 July 1915:

The Commissioner of Police has informed the Council that the total extinction of street lighting, when warning is received of an impending attack by hostile aircraft, is *most undesirable* . . . and would rather aggravate than reduce the degree of danger to which the public are exposed. Fire Brigades would not be able to reach their destinations, ambulance and police movements would be hindered, and all the elements of panic would be introduced. The Admiralty are satisfied that the present system of reduced lighting is the more satisfactory condition, since an observer from the sky is quite unable to determine the quarter of London he is passing over.

All these police objections seem to have been forgotten by the time Hitler's War came, and we shuffled about in the inky blackness of the first few months with our little shrouded pocket torches. It may have been true enough in 1915 that 'an observer from the sky' wouldn't know what part of London he was bombing, but everyone living near a bomb-site told everyone else, with a pride that it was hurtful to challenge, that 'they were after the gasometer', the steelworks, the barracks, even the school or the hospital.

In 1915 you could buy little luminous or light-reflecting buttons for wearing in the dark streets, but although someone bought one for Annie she wouldn't wear it: I suppose she thought it had been designed specifically for her, and she did not wish to be an oddity. Her supposed helplessness in the dark would have merited some study in itself, for on winter evenings she sometimes seemed to anticipate the air-raids, beginning to twitter and mumble to herself long before the gas warning came. We had neighbours who maintained that their pet dogs were similarly prescient, whining and fidgeting an hour or more before an air raid warning alerted their owners. I always found this hard to believe until one day, hurrying home in the dusk from somewhere with Annie and Roland, I heard a horse and cart behind us—a long way behind—and was surprised to hear Annie exclaim: 'There! That's the coalman, and no one at home. Come on, hurry.' How did *she* know it was the coal cart? We didn't. Even if she had turned round to look (and she didn't) it was by then too dark to see at that distance what kind of cart it was. I discovered that she *smelled* that coal cart. (I discovered, too, but not until many years later, that what she smelled was not the coal but the Swedish tar on the sacks. In the intervening years I never did understand why coal smelled so wonderful on the cart and stopped smelling of anything as soon as it had been delivered.) I am not saying that poor deaf Annie could similarly smell distant Zeppelins, only that she may have had sharpened perceptions of which we knew nothing.

If the war had begun for me with any kind of patriotic excitement and vicarious heroism, the stuffing was knocked out of it all by what happened to the Comerton family. My school friend Roland Comerton had an elder brother whose strange first name was Ashe and who, at just under eighteen years of age, had got into the Royal Navy in 1911 or 1912. In November 1914 he was serving in the armoured cruiser *Monmouth* at the Battle of Coronel, off the coast of Chile. Rear-Admiral Sir

Christopher Cradock's flagship, the *Good Hope*, went out of control and blew up with a huge explosion. Not a man survived. The *Glasgow* and the *Monmouth*, both on fire, limped away into the growing darkness, but the totally defenceless *Monmouth* was easily overtaken by the German *Nürnberg*—and then given a chance to surrender. Surrender being refused, the *Monmouth* was promptly sunk by gunfire at point-blank range. As with the *Good Hope*, the whole ship's company died, for the sea was rough and the *Nürnberg*'s commander was unable to lower any boats for rescue. Among the junior officers on the *Nürnberg* was the son of Admiral Graf von Spee, Commander of the whole German squadron, and he later wrote: 'It was dreadful to have to fire on the poor devil, no longer able to defend herself; but her flag was still flying.'

I was at the time thoroughly shaken by this story, or by such details of it as we then knew. To me, and to the Comerton family, it meant that 500 or 600 young men had died by order of their own fat-headed Commander; who, I supposed, saw it as traditional and glorious to end their lives rather than surrender the ship and flag he couldn't possibly save. All those deaths accomplished absolutely nothing, and Ashe Comerton (whom, in fact, I had never known) became for me a frightful and symbolic condemnation of the whole evil, tub-thumping idiocy. An irrational consequence of this, which in retrospect I do not understand, was that instead of deciding that I was a pacifist I determined to get into the armed forces as soon as might be, on the lunatic reasoning that the bigger our forces became the quicker the war must end.

And it was in this frame of mind that I was taken from my Fulham playground, the Bishop's Park and the streets, the Library and the cinema and the beloved foreshore of the River Thames, and went to live in the City of London. It was now February 1916 and I was fourteen-and-a-half. What made 1916 my *annus mirabilis* was that I had finished, utterly finished, with school. But I didn't really know this until a week or two later.

7

THE CITY OF LONDON

What I did expect was a difficult time with my father, who was as determined that I should continue my schooling as I was resolved to have no more of it. Anyway it would have had to be a fee-paying school and, since I had failed my exam, the fees would have had to come from him. By the time I had children of my own I had often read with grim amusement the official educationist view that exam results were not to be seen as failures and successes but as convenient groupings arrived at by tests of inclination and need.

My father had already enquired about Christ's Hospital at Horsham, where the boys were all boarders and wore blue frock coats, knee breeches, and yellow stockings. I secretly rather fancied myself in these, and supposed in addition that Christ's Hospital *might* be something like Greyfriars, all kippers and toast, ragging and cricket. But although it is a City of London foundation (starting in Newgate Street in 1553), and my father seemed to expect that his City connection would accordingly be of some help, I was not eligible for a grant. He was not poor enough. It was the first time we had been adjudged too well off for something, and I was elated. It was also decisive.

However, for a few days after our arrival in the City there was no talk about school, though it was mid-February and not a holiday period. I was prepared for a bit of a row, in which I saw myself as striking a high-minded attitude about not battening upon my parents. This would maintain that, having failed in the general scholarship examination, I must now become a breadwinner, a support for the family and (I liked this bit) for the schooling of my gifted younger brother. I knew that the true reason for my resolution was not merely that I hated school but that I wanted (or thought I wanted) to get into the

Army: not the Navy, which I saw as a collection of coffin ships, nor the Royal Flying Corps, whose machines looked to me like big fragile kites of plywood and string. (For that matter, even today when I board a plane I try not to notice the fuselage, which still has the home-made look of something put together by a group of boys with a construction kit and some quick-setting glue.)

The move from Finsbury Park to Fulham in 1910 had been exciting enough, but we had had to admit that the pantechnicon van was pulled by horses. The move from Fulham to the City was done by a huge grey removals van (the very word pantechnicon was now being dismissed in the dictionaries as 'arch.') which was motor driven. Its engine was a De Dion Bouton. Its huge body protruded forward above the driver's cab, providing extra space now conveniently stuffed with our smaller belongings. The day of the move was bitterly cold and the roads and pavements were covered in hard-frozen snow. As we all watched, in greatcoats and muffled to the ears, until the last precious item had been crammed into the van, we were happily conscious that a few neighbours and some small child-ren were watching too, and we could hardly wait for them to see the real event of the day, the cranking up of the motor and its stirring into marvellous action. It started all right, but the rear wheels promptly skidded into the kerb with a bump that was echoed by alarming noises from inside. Sacks were put down under the rear wheels, the huge vehicle regained the crown of the road, and skidded again to the kerb with even worse noises inside. We were deeply mortified. Pride was ousted by embarrassment, joy by shame. But my father said there were two men inside the van, they would take care of every-thing; and we were to get ready for our Underground journey from Walham Green to Mansion House, the latter being the nearest station to our new residence at No. 1 College Hill.

No. 1 College Hill was the side entrance to a police station, which stood, and still stands, in Cloak Lane, near Cannon Street station in the City of London. An inconspicuous doorway, almost a hole-in-the-wall, opened on to a busy staircase running from basement to flat roof. On the iron stairs bustling and heavy-booted policemen ceaselessly pounded up and down, to and from ground floor Muster Room and basement Mess Room. One floor up, and overlooking both Cloak Lane and College Hill from corner windows, began our new, commodious, and oddly scattered six-roomed apartment on two floors. All the rooms must, I suppose, have been originally designed as administrative offices. On the arctic day of our arrival, Walter Hunt the Station housekeeper greeted us with what we came to recognize as effusiveness. A huge shambling figure in shirt-sleeves and very baggy trousers, he was a Constable selected for the job (from a lot of applicants) and supplied with accommodation in the building for himself and family. He had the quavering voice of someone perpetually on the verge of tears, and no one, it was said, had ever seen him smile. I came to know that he smiled by sending his eyebrows into his hair, and they were up there on the day of our arrival. It turned out that he was one of the kindest of men, with a tremendous respect for my father who, he never tired of insisting, was a born gentleman. Mr Hunt's special welcome that day was to have every room in the flat warmed by a roaring fire, and my brothers and I supposed (though not for long) that this would always be so and was one of the perks of the office. The most exciting thing about the whole place was that it was lit by electricity, and for the first time in my life I operated an electric-light switch. The wall-switches were all of brass, which today doesn't seem a very good idea, and the million-to-one certainty that pushing down a wall-switch would light up a room was sheer magic. We had 25 and 50 candle-power Ediswan lamps, 11 shillings a dozen (watts came later).

It was Walter Hunt who, I suppose, had as much influence on my life in the next few years as any two other men I've known; for he taught me to play billiards, and to play reasonably well. He taught me at the same time, unknowingly, the truth of Charles Roupell's complaint to Herbert Spencer that 'to play billiards well is a sign of an ill-spent youth'. It is idle to say, and yet I still say it, that I wish I could now have back the thousands of hours, aggregating no doubt several years of my life, that I have spent playing billiards, some of them hours of misery and self-disdain: I could now put them to so much better use.

The flat to which my father would normally have been entitled, but which had been allotted instead to the Detective Superintendent because it was suddenly ordained that he too should live inside the City boundaries, was a magnificent ten-roomed suite such as would satisfy most millionaires (who alone would be able to afford it). It would have been fine to have had that larger flat, but I can't remember that there was any heart-burning about it. If there was, it was assuaged by the discovery that the Detective Superintendent, a dapper, civilized and kindly man called John Ottaway, had five extremely attractive and nubile daughters who, despite a fiercely possessive and Scottish Calvinistic mother, were to play a significant part in our adolescent lives.

The problem of my own immediate future was confused by my own idiotic and, as it turned out, futile determination to get into Army uniform. Until about the middle of 1915 the recruiting offices for the Army (as distinct from the Navy and the RFC) were none too particular about the ages of likely-looking recruits presenting themselves, and were certainly not requiring birth certificates. But once the Lord Derby scheme was in operation, and before the shocking and gigantic casualties of Passchendaele, recruiting offices turned you away firmly and abruptly. Under-age boys lying about their birthdays and secretly enlisting had become an unmitigated nuisance. It had now been made easier for their parents to get them discharged, but the whole process was a waste of everyone's time. There were even threats of prosecution for falsely stating ages, though I cannot actually remember such a case going to court. My father knew, or anyway suspected, that I nonetheless had it in mind, and that whatever else might be effective for me in the way of counter-attraction it was unlikely to be school. Not even, I remember saying in one semi-tearful confrontation with my worried parents, the City of London School, about which there had to my own knowledge already been enquiries. (A couple of years later, when Roland was securely and happily installed there, I came to realize my stupidity.)

My father seemed unimpressed by what I saw as a providential discovery at that time, namely that in some parts of England and Wales the school-leaving age had been lowered from fourteen to eleven years, as a war-time emergency measure. If the war could justify the end of school for so many children at eleven, said I, how could it be right for a large lout like myself to continue after fifteen? Incidentally this particular war-time dispensation receives no mention whatever in most histories of the Kaiser's War. It is as if we all wanted to forget it. But I was prepared to exploit it vigorously at the time.

It all ended in my starting work in the rag-trade warehouse of Spreckley White & Lewis at 13/15 Cannon Street. 'Rag trade' was to me a quite new expression and I was horrified. I knew from what my mother had often told me that one of the 're-habilitation' jobs provided for its down-and-out protégés by the Salvation Army was rag-sorting. I believe it still is. Was I going to do that? Would I learn which rags were suitable for paper-making, which could be reprocessed for reincarnation as 'shoddy', and so on? I was soon apprised that 'rag trade' was a colloquialism for the dignified business of designing, making, and selling clothes, applied impartially to the swathing of those six-foot willowy models at Harrods and to the festooned market stalls of Petticoat Lane and the Portobello Road.

Spreckley White & Lewis were three elderly gentlemen who had inherited, from three even older ones of the same names, a thriving wholesale business of just that kind, and I was lucky (my father assured me) to be offered such an opening. The offer had come through a member of the City of London Special Constabulary who held my father in the kind of high esteem which rashly assumes all sons to be potentially as good as their fathers. He was called Mr Law, and I came to know that he was a cloth manufacturer who sold huge rolls of serge and gaberdine to my employers. I can still remember the sleepless nights that preceded the Monday morning on which I was to present myself at No. 13/15 Cannon Street, 'ask for Mr Sheears', and explain who I was. I am not sure what the position of Mr Sheears was, but I don't doubt that today he would be called personnel manager. He was a tiny white-haired man in a morning coat, whose mouth was entirely covered by a bushy white drooping moustache. The mouth, that is to say, was completely shrouded until he needed to speak very loudly or to take in a deep breath to sneeze with, the latter being frequently encouraged by huge pinches of snuff; and then he opened it wide and looked completely different. I was half frightened and half flattered to find that he was actually expecting me. He took me downstairs to the basement and the 'Entering Room', where I was to enter (in huge 'daybooks') the details of purchases made upstairs in the various departments by buyers from all the great dress emporia and fashion houses in the country. Making these entries and their related invoices, I sat all day in a kind of elevated pulpit in the far corner of the basement; and behind me, just the other side of a matchboard partition not constructed as a barrier against smells, were the lavatories used by such lowly staff members (including me) as were deemed to be adequately served by any sanitary system not officially condemned as lethal.

In those days I took some pride in my handwriting—in which, like both my brothers, I had carefully imitated my father. It must have commended itself to Mr White, the partner whose special area of concern was the Counting House. (You had to be a good penman to get into that sacred college of calligraphy, whose members greatly fancied themselves.) Within a few months I was translated to the Counting House, and remained there until after the period of this book. The firm of Spreckley White & Lewis survived the two world wars and came to an end about 1950; but the Kaiser's War had been in progress for eighteen months when I joined the firm in 1916, and I have no conception of its atmosphere in time of peace. Yet I remember little about it that could be called a wartime memory, and indeed its solid and long-established routines induced one to forget for long periods that there was a war going on anywhere.

I started at £40 a year—which at that time wasn't bad. My father ordained that I was to have the whole of my fifteen shillings a week for myself, plus my board and lodging and plus 'some help' in the buying of clothes. I was staggered by all this at first, but came to know that his object was twofold. First, to give me some independence, a complete change of regimen, and something to wean me from the besotted contemplation of myself as a soldier. He knew about soldiering, and I could take it from him, my son, that I wouldn't like it for more than about an hour. He used to say, perhaps ambiguously, that he had never seen anyone like me in the Army anyway. Secondly, to appease the conscience which told him continually (and wrongly) that he was weak in letting me leave school—and save him so much money. Bless you, my dear father, if I could but choose again I would go to school. But what then . . . ?

Spreckley's was a firm in whose service any honest and reasonably intelligent person could find a niche for life and settle down, happily enough, as a responsible citizen with satisfying leisure pursuits, a decent lawn mower and a family. In the Counting House I wrote letters to customers and manufacturers in the 'copperplate' script, downstrokes-thick-upstrokes-thin, which I suppose had really begun to die out with the dissolution of the monasteries but was taking a long time about it. It was finally killed off, of course, by the ball-point pen. I used a Waverley nib, to which I had been introduced by my father. There were only two possible nibs, he said, the Waverley and the Times, and he always preferred a Times (he was a fine penman, imitated assiduously by my brothers and myself). My own preference for the gentler response of the Waverley owed nothing to the famous little jingle to be seen on advertisement hoardings everywhere:

> They come as a boon and a blessing to men—
> The Pickwick, the Owl and the Waverley pen.

Indeed I had never known anyone to use a Pickwick or an Owl, or even heard of anyone who knew such a person. But the custom of the time was to make a page of handwriting look as nearly as possible like an 'illuminated manuscript'; and although it must now seem a leisurely way of doing business, no one seemed to mind how long it took to make a business letter into a work of art. Incidentally those letters often acquired an odd appearance by being 'pressed' in an old-fashioned copying machine, from which they emerged wringing wet and were crammed into their envelopes, still wet, by junior clerks anxious to get home. Some years later I worked for a chartered accountant who, as well as auditing his clients' affairs, provided the service of 'writing up' their books (the true esoteric meaning of 'accountancy'). And there I spent much time decorating the heavy cartridge-paper leaves of Share Ledgers and Capital Account Books with the machine-like script I had taught myself from copy-books. It seems odd, now that the term 'hand-made' has come to denote a departed excellence (all too often a phoney nostalgic self-deception), that we should have striven in those days to make our handwriting look 'beautifully' mechanical.

In the counting house we sat at very high desks fitted with footrails, and accordingly we had high stools with padded leather seats and bits of kapok protruding untidily from gashes in their sides. Why, I used to wonder, did we not have desks the same height as an ordinary table, and chairs to match? In the illustrations to Dickens, Bob Cratchit, Mr Wemmick, and all the other clerks were always depicted on high stools. Charles Lamb worked on a high stool at the East India Office. Perhaps in those days there was some reason why they must all get their feet off the floor—cold draughts, mice, rats, damp? Some of my contemporaries hold today that the height of office stools and desks was determined by the need to work much of the time standing up, and the fact that your hands and elbows could thus remain at the same height standing or sitting. And why did you need to work standing up? Because more often than not you were using two ledgers side by side, or a ledger and a day-book; and these were always so huge—often the size of a bound-up quarter's *Times*—that the clerk moved to the book more easily than the book to the clerk. Moreover books wore out more quickly than clerks, and were less expendable. So you slipped off the stool to consult whichever book wasn't actually in front of you as you perched. If this is right (and it leaves open the question why the books couldn't have been smaller), why did all the pubs have high stools at a high bar, and why do all the neon-lit, neo-marzipan pubs of today continue the tradition? Again, it is said, to recognize and propitiate that Anglo-Saxon phenomenon, the perpendicular boozer. 'Imagine yourself,' said an earnest drinker to me, 'going into a pub where all the beer-mugs had to be stood on ordinary tables. Where the hell would you put your elbow?'

The ledgers and daybooks, all leather-bound, had been in heavy use for so many years that all their covers were powdering—as any old leather-bound book will powder when roughly used. Their constant opening and banging shut had deposited a fine dust over everything by the end of the day; and one of my clearest recollections of that counting house is that everyone working in it, including myself in due course, kept his own clothes-brush for use at two minutes before going-home time. At that daily moment there occurred a concerted and vigorous brushing of jackets and trousers, some men even brushing inside their permanent turn-ups. I came to suspect that this sibilant outburst of brush-wielding was really designed to announce the time of day to our elderly and somnolent chief cashier Mr Edwards, who might otherwise work abstractedly on and whose decision alone could bring our working day to a close. (Mr Edwards's high stool, by the way, had a little back to it.) Unexpectedly, my mother had some difficulty in understanding why I needed a clothes-brush at the office: I never used one at home. Angrily, I bought one of my own. This office competitiveness in the matter of smart appearance reminded me that at school a few years before, my form master, who was always clearing out boys' books from his shelves at home, frequently offered a book for 'the smartest boy of the week'. It was usually a Manville Fenn, a Captain F. S. Brereton, a Mayne Reid, or a Talbot Baines Reade. There was intense competition.

Sometimes he offered instead an old clockwork engine or a boxwood spinning-top.

I suppose that about the most useless (and therefore the least perishable) mental lumber remaining from those days is the names of hundreds of rag-trade retailers who were customers of Spreckley White & Lewis. They are called up by nearly every mention of an English place-name: Parsons and Hart of Andover, Kennards of Croydon, Priddis of Streatham, Bobby's of Bournemouth, Bulls of Reading, Lewis's of Manchester. They play their part in my strictly private system of associative geography by which any place-name in the world (if I know where it is) lights up a little brain-cell with a local picture.

At about this time it was decided that I should have my very first made-to-measure suit. It was to be made by an old friend of the family, Mr C. Dell of Dawes Road, Fulham, who put himself forward as a Bespoke Tailor. I was very excited at this prospect, but in order to be as excited as possible I wanted to know what happened to an ordinary tailor when he was Bespoke. If you bespeak something, said my father (and his dictionary), you order it in advance. But I wasn't bespeaking a tailor, I said, I was bespeaking a suit of clothes. Moreover shouldn't the word be Bespoken, and why was it only tailors—not shoemakers and hatters and coffin-makers—who were thus described? Did you ever hear of a Bespoke Builder and Decorator? No answers were forthcoming, either at home or in the little fitting-room of Mr C. Dell, who always looked rather like Mr H. G. Wells with an inch-tape round his neck. But the blue serge, pin-stripe suit I had bespoke turned out to be so profoundly satisfying that all further questioning seemed ungrateful. It felt rich and luxurious and it cost three guineas. I took it back to the City in a cardboard box with 'C. Dell, Bespoke Tailor' printed on it, tried it on in front of the family, and for most of the evening stood about in a variety of attitudes rather than sit down and begin pulling it out of shape. Then I learned that it had been bought, not for 'best' but for me to wear to the office: my father had been thinking I looked shabby.

This was the more generous because the question of what I should wear to the office had just been the theme of an earth-shaking row. My father was a man with an unusual number of blind spots, gaps in a superficially impressive *savoir faire*. For many years he had owned a morning coat, which he never wore, an awe-inspiring affair with tails. He must have bought it for some extra-special and non-recurrent occasion. Now, it probably upbraided him every time he opened his wardrobe door. He decided suddenly that it would be quite suitable for a young man to wear in an office, especially a counting house; and he had already tried to impose it on my brother Harold, now working in the counting house at W. H. Smith & Sons in the Strand. Harold had at first laughed dutifully, though a bit nervously (we were very loyal about our father's little jokes), but when at last he was reluctantly convinced that the 'old man' was serious, he turned white to the lips. In vain did he plead that in a morning coat he would be the laughing stock of the whole building and, probably, of the entire length of the Strand. He went so far as to put the thing on, and stand with his arms half-lifted to show how ridiculous it made him look. The absurd argument went on and on until at last he had made it desperately clear that he was ready to leave home if that was the only solution. My father then gave in and left the room very seriously disgruntled.

But far from vanquished. Having found me the job at Spreckley's, he was now anxious that I should do him justice both in performance (which I never did) and in clerkly appearance (which he was doing his best to ruin). Out came the dreaded frock coat again. How and why it could be thought suitable for someone like me I shall never understand, but once again it was produced with a pride that seemed still to be undimmed as the 'proper business wear' for a promising young man. Some awful fascination made me consent to put it on and, having got thus far, hurry to my parents' bedroom where there was a full-length mirror. One glance in this, screwing round to get a glimpse of my own rear, brought incredulity to the verge of tears. After a few moments to collect myself, I strode back to say that rather than appear in public in such a garment I would take the King's Shilling. (I was rather fond of this phrase at the time. It dated from the Victorian practice of giving an Army recruit a shilling when he was sworn in and I thought it sounded rather good.) The row began. Did I suppose, demanded my father, that I knew more about suitable city dress than he did? Yes (gulp), I supposed I did. Indeed? Was I perhaps forgetting that he was earning his living, and observing what people were wearing, before I was born? That, I offered, seemed to be the trouble. Oh, it went on and on. It ended as abruptly as Harold's battle of two or three years before, probably because my father suddenly reminded himself that I was still starry-eyed about the Army, and could easily be goaded or bored into joining up by mis-stating my age. I don't know what happened to the morning coat, but I like to think that it went, perhaps by way of some jumble sale, to a street trader who would wear it when selling matches.

The whole sad affair ended in the happy denouement of the three-guinea bespoke suit. For some weeks at the office I worked standing up in this, fearful of shining the trousers on the padded stool. And when it came to 5.28 p.m. every day, no one was more assiduous than I in wielding the clothes-brush and coaxing my little clouds of dust from the three-guinea trousers. I think we all probably brushed the nap off new clothes in a matter of weeks.

Across the narrow little lane called College Hill our sitting-room window looked straight into that of Dick Whittington's house—or so we were always told, though a number of buildings along College Hill claimed to have housed him, and the existing blue plaque on one of them, proclaiming that 'The house of Richard Whittington, Mayor of London, stood on this site 1423', is believed by many to be mistaken. But if he was in bed there on Sunday mornings and hoping for a lie-in he would probably have been awakened, I hope more tolerantly than I, by the 6.30 a.m. bell of St. Michael Paternoster Royal a few doors down the hill (now a marvellous Wren church with the old mediaeval crypt still intact); and he would have been kept awake by it through a succession of short morning services until he despaired and got up. But at least it was to be his burial place, and in deference to the Whittington story it used to have a mummified cat in the church wall.

My daily walks to and from Spreckley's in Cannon Street were always during the rush hour, and the traffic congestion was usually worse than anything the impatient Londoner has put up with at any time since then—especially, and to me inexplicably, on a wet Friday. Motor vehicles were becoming commonplace. Unless they were in some way eccentric, like Mr Solly Joel's famous and noiseless electric brougham or some such exciting foreign automobile as the Isotto-Fraccini, the Darracq, or the Hispano-Suiza, they no longer turned many heads. They were all subject to a maximum speed limit of twenty miles an hour, and in some districts (though not in the City) there were local limits as low as five. Motor buses were limited to twelve, but in the City they had little chance to attain even that. At this time they were 'Old Bill' buses, the model famous for its use in France by the Army Service Corps as troop transport. These seemed to me at the time, and still seem, about the ugliest vehicles ever designed since the advent of the wheel. They were greatly mistrusted by some of the road safety authorities; and by way of example I recently found in the Minutes of the Fulham Borough Council for 1 November 1911 a complaint about motor omnibuses and their 'damage to roadways, vibration, serious annoyance to inhabitants, positive danger to premises along the route, and loss of rates from premises vacated by victims'. Motor buses had first appeared in London in 1905, and their drivers were often prosecuted for dangerous driving by racing—'Vanguards' (petrol driven) versus 'metropolitan' (steam) buses. The Old Bill buses were fitted with a so-called lifeguard between front and rear wheels on each side, an arrangement of wooden slats angled so as to deflect outwards, and clear of the back wheels, anyone falling against the side of the bus. I never understood what it did to anyone run over by a front wheel, but preferred not to think of that.

Except along the broad Victoria Embankment, where they

were confined to the river side of the roadway, tramcars had never been allowed into the City of London. The rails carrying these wonderful and lamented vehicles came to an abrupt end at various points round the City boundary—Grays Inn Road, Hatton Garden, Farringdon Street, Bishopsgate, and Southwark Bridge. Horse-drawn vehicles abounded everywhere, mixed incongruously with the growing throng of motor buses, taxicabs, and lorries. As I walked through narrow thoroughfares like Carter Lane, Knightrider Street, and Bread Street I was always astounded at the skill of the carmen navigating heavy pair-horsed wagons in those confined spaces: they had the advantage that they could turn in their own length, the front wheels turning right in beneath the undercarriage. The stumbling horses seemed always to help intelligently and willingly in the process, and almost able to do it unaided; there was little use of the whip and not much shouting. Fallen horses were, however, a frequent sight. And once down, they were seldom able to get up while still in the shafts, and there was a general traffic hold-up while they were released from the harness, scrambled up with a clatter of iron shoes, and stood waiting patiently to be re-harnessed. I believe there was much cruelty to horses in those days, on the part of owners and carmen in whom the only emotions kindled by a horse were anger and impatience. And there were City policemen, usually ex-cavalrymen, who were horsey experts as well as born prosecutors, and who spent most of their time at the magistrates' courts waiting for some cruelty case to be called on, while the ill-treated horse waited in the yard outside, with protruding haunch-bones or one hoof held limply.

There were said to be 250,000 horses in daily use in London at that time, and they varied from the magnificent Flanders mares pulling brewers' drays to the spindle-shanked, nodding seniors who wearily tugged the growlers still used by 'town' commercial travellers. One of these waited daily in Bread Street outside my employers' premises until the Spreckley 'traveller' was ready to load it with his samples—mantles, skirts, furs, and costumes. There were still horse-drawn cabs at the railway stations and even a few hansoms. And there was a roving army of semi-vagrants who earned a precarious living by holding the heads of horses while their drivers were, for reasons good and not so good, absent from the scene.

It was also the heyday of the box-tricycle, a vehicle which seems to have been born a little before I was, and which was then much used in the City for the delivery of office towels, stationery, office-cleaning materials, and butchers' sundries, and (in summer) for the sale of ice-cream. The more common sort comprised a cog-and-chain driving wheel behind a swivelling box on two wheels, but a more interesting version had the rider in front, standing on the pedals (probably scorning a saddle) in front of the carrier-box. At the rear was a small swivelling wheel. Steering was done, I think, by buttock, and accidents were sufficiently frequent to make the whole thing a worthwhile adventure for the kind of youth in charge. The box-tricycle boys lived hardly less dangerously than the van-boys (Carter Patersons, Pickfords, etc.) whose *raison d'être* was a London traffic law which forbade anyone to leave a horse (with or without a van) unattended and liable to stray, or to take fright and bolt. The van-boy hoisted himself on to the tailboard by means of a rope swinging from the roof of the van; but not until the van was actually in motion, because swinging up on to a merely stationary van would look unprofessional. This involved sufficient misjudgements and injuries to establish the routine as inviolable. There were Post Office messenger boys, Theatre Agency boys, 'licensed messenger' boys, boys from Reuters Press Agency, shoeblacks and street orderly boys; all of whom have been displaced by the motor vehicle, the telephone, and (in the case of the shoeblacks) by the evolution of fancy footwear that couldn't be cleaned at the roadside.

And they all whistled beautifully. Oh, it may be that the passage of the years has lent enchantment to their vanished sound, and much of the noise they made was probably awful. It may be that the melodies then were better for whistling. Ivor Novello was turning out memorable tunes by the dozen,

Nat D. Ayer had got everyone humming and whistling his *Bing Boys* (pre-eminently 'If You Were the Only Girl in the World'), and two young men called Felix Powell and George Asaf had provided us all, in the desperate mood of the time, with 'Pack Up Your Troubles in Your Old Kit Bag and Smile, Smile, Smile'. As everyone knows, this was to some extent used by the British Army as a marching song, but the soldiers generally preferred the lugubrious 'There's a Long, Long Trail A-winding', which (like 'Tipperary') made the French ask each other why the British Expeditionary Force marched about France singing in a manner *toujours si triste*. It was in 1909 that I first heard a piano-organ playing 'Tipperary', although in fact it came out the year before.

The youth who operated the shaky hydraulic lift at Spreckley's (he pulled on a corner rope that passed through it vertically) was always whistling the better-known arias from *Carmen*, and he was very good at it. When I found that all the street boys were also whistling *Carmen* I asked him one day what was going on, and learned that everyone was going to see a Cecil B. de Mille movie of the opera and then buying gramophone records of the music. *Chu Chin Chow* had started its five-year run at His Majesty's Theatre, adding 'The Cobbler's Song' and 'The Robbers' March' to millions of whistling repertoires. I remembered a milk roundsman in Gowan Avenue in the early mornings who, as he rattled his lidded pint and quart cans, unfailingly—and perfectly—whistled his way through the whole of the Delibes *Naïla* Waltz. Where have all the whistlers gone, and why? Do we all, like Cassius, think too much? Dryden presents his Cymon as a mindless bumpkin, who

> Trudged along unknowing what he sought
> And whistled as he went, for want of thought.

But even Cymon, once he had fallen in love, came to recognize his own oafishness and gave up whistling. Today, nearly everyone has given up whistling.

The 'street orderly boys' of the City, some of whom in fact were middle-aged men, were a company of peak-capped labourers, employed by the City Corporation's Street Cleansing Department. They kept the City streets cleaner than any I have since seen in any part of the world, and certainly cleaner than London (or indeed Britain) has been since the Litter Act of 1959 made it criminal to leave muck lying around. On wet days these expert scavengers, working in teams, performed one particular feat which few of its privileged spectators can ever have forgotten, and which really merited a background of film music. Pushing giant 'squeegees' and moving in echelon, they transferred oceans of mud from the roadway into the gutters and then guided it into the drains, in successful defiance of the densest traffic. (On a dry day they used wide scoops and shovelled the refuse into three-wheeled barrows.) Why, and I am asking without regret, is there no such mud today? Was all of it really caused by the horses?

The City streets, mostly composed of blocks of tarred wood, were watered and swept every night; and at five o'clock in the morning the air was cleaner and sweeter than you could have supposed possible in any built-up area. My father nourished a semi-proprietary satisfaction in this, and for a year or two my brothers and I were content to take his word for it, feeling no urge to get up and sniff for ourselves at 5 a.m. But then one summer I began sometimes getting up in time to take a bus ride to Hyde Park (twopence on the No. 9 from Mansion House Station), swim in the Serpentine (among elderly cranks who did it all the winter too), and be back in time for breakfast, all in an hour and a half. I believe I enjoyed it, but one excuse for introducing the subject here is that during those war years Hyde Park north of the Serpentine was occupied by enormous flocks of sheep, which became so inured to the presence of human beings that the two species intermingled, I was going to say indistinguishably.

It is pertinent at this point to say that this voluntary spurt of early rising was about to receive a shocking and statutory setback. Mr William Willett, our friend the master-printer in Bow Lane, had been campaigning since about 1908 to impose 'daylight saving' on us all by Act of Parliament. What he wanted to do was to advance clock-time in four steps, each of twenty minutes, on the first four Sundays in April, thus extending the day by 80 minutes after the fourth Sunday. Then in September, a counter-motion of 20 minutes each on four Sundays' clock-time would make the clocks agree once again with Greenwich mean time. It was all too complicated, and in 1908 a Committee of Parliament amended the proposal to one alteration of one hour in April and September. Then it was turned down because of the 'serious inconvenience' it must cause to many people—farmers, railways, the fishing industry, the theatre, the Stock Exchange. There were Daylight Saving Bills every year, all of them getting first readings only. Then in May 1916 Sir Henry Norman revived the idea as 'a means of saving artificial lighting', the Government supported him, and as the Summer Time Act it became law on 17 May. Our City MP, Sir Frederick Banbury, was very cross. 'Suppose I *don't* put my clock forward?' he said in the Commons on 8 May. 'Is there to be a penalty? The Government ought not to take advantage of a time of war to juggle with the hands of a clock.' And the *Daily Chronicle* had a cartoon showing Mr Herbert Samuel, Home Secretary, tossing up clock hands and catching them. Two saner comments of the time are worth recalling. Mr John St. Loe Strachey, editor of *The Spectator*:

We make a great mistake in lying in bed when the sun is shining outside. . . . The solution of those who say 'Then why don't you act on your own principles? The remedy is in your own hands' is a delusion. The busy man must keep the same hours as other people.

And Mr Winston Churchill, then First Lord of the Admiralty:

The measure simply proposes to substitute a convenient for an inconvenient standard of artificial time. . . . The Admiral commanding one of the battle squadrons has successfully introduced the daylight saving principle in his fleet. He makes all possible use of the daylight without any consciousness of getting up earlier than usual and without altering the fleet routine.

My father, who was against it from the first and never changed his mind, produced an argument which astonished me, especially since he was deeply interested in astronomy (his bedside book for years was Sir Robert Ball's *The Story of the Heavens*, and we had all dutifully listened to longish readings from it). It might be a convenience, he said, to have the same time as France, but it wasn't really acceptable to have the same time as Germany. And he also thought that for the man in Penzance 12 noon was 'Greenwich Mean Time', and he would never accept that even the man in Penzance was pretending that 11.40 was 12 noon merely because he didn't want to be an odd-man-out. The pro-and-anti correspondence in the newspapers was enormous: you would never have thought a world war was in progress. And from among my own friends and colleagues I cannot remember one who was in favour of the change. Everyone foresaw chaos.

*

It was at about this time that there occurred two wholly dissimilar events which significantly changed the course of my life. One was that my brother Harold fell in love with the girl next door. The other was that my parents acquired a very peculiar armchair, so designed that the occupant, once installed with a book, could hardly get out again and thus found himself reading books he would normally lay aside. Let me try first to describe the condition of my brother, which seemed to me at once startling, enviable, and pathetic.

I have already referred to the five beautiful daughters of Mr John Ottaway, the Detective Superintendent who occupied the more commodious flat next door. The second oldest was Doris, pretty rather than beautiful, and one of those girls in whom Nature pleasingly contrives to mingle the pretty with the sturdy. She had, for example, rather solid-looking legs and very square shoulders. She might have been invented by Angela Brazil; she personified, as it were, hockey and cocoa. She also had freckles, which I regard as highly dangerous, and she had the kind of charm that would melt a snowman in thirty seconds, starting from the top. Harold met her in the oddest way, and the fateful encounter belongs exactly in the period.

Whenever there was a night-time Zeppelin raid, which in 1916 and 1917 was pretty frequently, our two families, the Ottaways and the Hewitts, went downstairs and crowded into one of the police-station cells. These had arched ceilings and walls about two feet thick, and were considered safe. (In Hitler's War twenty-five years later, a direct hit on the Station showed tragically that they were not.) They were, however, insulated against the noise of guns and bombs. And we had earlier warning of the imminence of air raids than the general public. Anti-aircraft guns on lorries tore through the streets, stopping every so often to fire at the sky—and the explosions, apart from breaking many windows, would nearly shake down an ordinary house. We hardly heard them. There was a gun on the high-level footbridge of the Tower Bridge, I suppose about the flimsiest gun-emplacement imaginable. Its flash and roar seemed tremendous if you were out of doors, but in our communal cell we heard it not at all. The 'Air Raid Precautions Service' in most parts of London, certainly in Fulham and (Cousin Florrie told us) in Finsbury Park, was a do-it-yourself affair. Red and green lights were fixed to lamp-posts at main street junctions. The green light showed until raiders were on the way, and then the red light came on. Voluntary street wardens were appointed by the residents—there was no government sponsorship, control, interference or, it seemed, concern. The volunteer wardens took it in turns to watch for the warning light. When it changed to red they went round the streets knocking at doors where the householders had chalked a 'W' on the wall to show that they belonged. (Soon after the war, a letter 'W' in your window meant that you wanted a visit from a man riding a box tricycle and bringing Walls' Ice Cream.) In the City we knew little of all this, but we reckoned to know a lot about bombs.

For some hours at a time we three boys would thus be thrown together with the five girls, not to mention the two mums. Connie, the oldest, was already engaged to marry, but the others were unattached, and there took place some more or less inevitable pairing of the kind which doesn't usually outlast the special circumstances. In Harold's case it did, and I had my first close-up vision of a young man who was not only seriously, indeed frantically, in love but determined to intensify his condition. He never did this kind of thing by halves, and this one he did madly and extravagantly. His daily deportment for the next five years could have been adequately described and interpreted only by Dostoevsky, Colette, and P. G. Wodehouse working as a drafting committee.

Taking the Ottaway girls in order of diminishing age and height, the next one down was Phyllis, who was 15, had gentle eyes, a wide smile, and very long brown hair in thick plaits. It seemed to me a very flattering arrangement that she should voluntarily pair up with me, and it was rather fostered by the watchful Mrs Ottaway, who was well aware of what was developing between Harold and Doris, saw safety in foursomes, and regarded me as totally expendable except as a kind of ball and chain. Doubtless to Harold's disgust, the four of us for some time went everywhere together—concerts, walks, cinemas, picnics, church. For many years I had taken my elder brother as an exemplar in 'all the changing scenes of life'. Whatever he did, I did or tried to do. The condition of being in love was familiar enough in all the books I was now reading. The maidens fallen in love with were all about my age. Louise de la Vallière, as an example, was sixteen, Shakespeare's Juliet fourteen. Accordingly, I decided, this development was important and I must give it proper scope. I would fall in love with Phyllis. After all, she was rather beautiful, had what seemed to me an exquisite speaking voice (for me, a *sine qua non*), and not merely allowed me to put my arm round her shoulders on the tops of buses but actually responded by putting her head on my shoulder.

But my 'walking out' episode with Phyllis was fairly brief, probably because I was too often reading and didn't want to go out unless there was somewhere to go. I believe I was a bit of a bore, still probably talking a little like the front page of *John Bull* and seeming to know rather a lot, or anyway wanting to seem like it. I remember her saying once: 'Well, you do have such strong views about everything, don't you?'; and if I could but recall what the word 'Well' linked up with, I should probably have the lost clue to the break-up. But once this had happened it became possible to study Harold's condition objectively; and whereas I had uneasily felt, hitherto, that this might have bordered on the scatty, I now saw that it had crossed the border and left it far behind. Sad to say, what eventually happened was that a year or two later Doris fell in love with somebody else and Harold was turned down. He took it very badly and in fact had quite a serious breakdown; recovering from which, he resolutely blued all the money he had saved in four years for his marriage; and apart from equipping himself (handsomely) with all the suits and shirts he had been going without, he brought home an enormous quantity of gramophone records, including the nine symphonies of Beethoven, giving Roland and me such a feast as we could never otherwise have known. We were sorry about Doris, but her defection gave us limitless consequential pleasure. We each had different favourites among the Beethoven symphonies, though we loved them all: Harold the Ninth, Roland the Fifth, myself the Seventh. But in deciding these preferences we wore those records thin, even with fibre needles carefully sharpened by hand.

The fabulous armchair was newly acquired after our move to the City, I know not where or why. Its horrible chocolate brown imitation leather (I think it was called Rexine) was commonplace enough, but its slippery seat was tilted back at a grotesque angle, probably at least 45 degrees. There was thus no way of half-sitting in it. Anyone trying to sit forward with, say, a cup of tea was attempting the impossible: you simply slid down until you hit the back. Accordingly no one ever sat in it but myself. It became my chair. And in it, mainly because I couldn't get out, I read all the novels (borrowed from the policemen's Divisional Library downstairs) of Bulwer Lytton, Harrison Ainsworth, Charles Lever, Scott, Stevenson, Fenimore Cooper, and Alexandre Dumas. I don't believe anyone would read those, I mean all of them, unless he were held down by gravitation in a chair from which escape had to be so carefully planned.

At the same time there came a revived craze at home for Pitman's Shorthand, largely because my father, whose interest in it had never flagged, began buying not only the *Phonographic Weekly* but the Isaac Pitman editions of famous novels transcribed into shorthand. He began with Conan Doyle's *The Sign of Four*, and there soon appeared *The Vicar of Wakefield, Robinson Crusoe*, and (believe it or not) a complete shorthand version of the King James Bible. Almost certainly because of the chair, I read them all—learning a great deal in the process about the pronunciation of biblical proper names. I doubt that, but for this, I should ever have read either *The Vicar of Wakefield* or *Crusoe*, to say nothing of reading through the entire Bible. But one evening, during a visit by our beloved Cousin Florrie (still living at Finsbury Park), she challenged me to read out a passage from *Robinson Crusoe*, putting her finger on it at random. She didn't know shorthand, and I could possibly have bluffed her; but she *did* know her Robinson Crusoe and it would have been risky. Little did any of us foresee what this simple act was going to involve. She had picked on the passage where Man Friday, comparing his own God with Crusoe's, had asked 'Why God no kill Devil?' and the embarrassed Crusoe, having first affected not to hear, then told the poor fellow that 'We are all preserved to repent and be pardoned', and that you must have a Devil to tempt you into the deeds calling for Divine forgiveness. Man Friday then came up with the problem that had long been worrying me: 'So you, me, Devil, all wicked, all preserved, all repent, God pardon all?' Actually I felt that my chances of pardon were about the same as Friday's.

But there followed a dangerous discussion with my parents and Cousin Florrie about the Devil as a real presence, a Someone, a personification of evil. My father, as ever, got out his dictionary. 'The Evil One,' he said, 'the personification of evil.' And he announced, rather than suggested, that if we believed in Christ, as the personification of good, we had no logical escape from a belief in the Devil, the anti-Christ. Without the Devil there was no virtue in being good, because you couldn't be anything else. Cousin Florrie's view always was that the Devil was not the source or principle of evil, he was the promoter and organizer of it. Evil existed in the gaps between deeds of good, it was the negation of good and nothing could come of it unless it was organized.

I understood and believed little of it, and I can remember my mother's troubled face as she heard me sullenly saying so. When the time came for Cousin Florrie to leave, I walked with her to the Bank Underground station. 'Don't worry about the difficult things in the Bible,' she said in her comfortable voice. 'Your father is the best of men, but you can never argue with him. He will only grow angry and threatening.' And at one time she would have been right about the threatening, but he had lately taken to subjecting me to Good Influences. A few years earlier he had always told me that 'if my ways didn't mend' he would have me sent to an Industrial School. If my conduct had been outstandingly bad he would make this a Reformatory School, which I understood to be rather worse, something designed for boys of truly depraved character. In 1933 these dread institutions were abolished by the good old English legislative process of enacting that they were to be called something else: they became Approved Schools, themselves to be abolished in 1969 by being called Community Homes. But in those days you could get there by being hauled in front of a Juvenile Court at the behest of a parent or guardian who complained in writing that you were 'beyond his control'. Because I could never quite see my father publicly avowing that anyone or anything was beyond his control, even if it was, I never really took this threat very seriously. But whenever arguments arose on matters of ethics or morals, it could be called into use as a conversation-stopper.

The policy of exposing me to Good Influences had been partially served by the prolonged episode of Mr Herbert. But soon after we had moved to the City Mr Herbert and his marvellous piano-playing daughter had gone to live in Wiltshire, where in 1917 he died. A need had already become generally apparent (though not, at this stage, to me) that I should be once again within the influence of some kind of church or chapel. I was not in the least dismayed at the idea, since I had now begun to feel isolated at weekends (the City at weekends is like a city of the dead), and I saw in this proposal a chance of meeting people who could not merely be buddies but could be introduced at home without the wearisome business of establishing their *bona fides*. As church or chapel members they would, believe it or not, rank as Verified Characters. Harry Woolsey, a long-established friend of my Fulham schooldays, was now almost my sole link with Fulham, where he was to some extent identified with the 'social activities' at Munster Park Wesleyan Methodist Church. I told him of the parental wish that I should get similarly involved somewhere, and he rather shockingly disclosed that he was on the verge of giving it all up in bewilderment. In the course of a long (and familiar) walk to Richmond Park one Saturday afternoon and evening we decided to support each other on a round of the alternative Services provided on Sunday evenings by Christian churches of as many denominations as we could think of.

We started with a Quaker meeting in what had once been a cookshop in the Fulham Road, where we sat in astonished silence, and supposed that we had in some way been in touch with the Infinite. I remember that we were given an un-fussy but warmly affectionate welcome by the Quakers and decided to go again. A week or two later we tried Evensong at West-minster Abbey, where it was difficult to encompass the idea that the same God was being worshipped (it seemed, rather, that this one was being sumptuously propitiated). Then the Salvation Army in Dawes Road, Fulham, which would have been a heart-warming experience but for the perfervid inter-jections, the strange gestures and posturings, of the more dedicated soldiers. This meeting had a band which comprised about ten or a dozen brass instruments and was excruciatingly bad. (But later I went to Salvation Army services in Regents Hall, London, where the band was magnificent.) A churchful of earnest Anglicans near Hammersmith Broadway was similarly embarrassing: to both of us, in our questing mood, there was something repugnant and powerfully unsettling about religious ecstasy. Nothing, we felt, could more effectively make a chap feel that he 'didn't belong'. It was the same with a Christadelphian Church at Parsons Green, where the atmosphere was one of controlled hysteria, members of the congregation shouting 'Allelujah' and 'Praise the Lord' even more loudly than the Salvationists did, but seeming less happy about it. We were overawed at Brompton Oratory, and faintly surprised to find its members singing hymns that we knew well. We found an Elim Pentecostal Four Square Gospel Mission in (I think) Chelsea, and were frightened by a sermon of sweeping condemnation and dark prophecy. There was a little Mission, unattached so far as I know, at a place called Twynholme Hall in Lillie Road, Fulham (it is now a Baptist Church), where you could feel, as you sat among the rows of artisans and their wives, that if religion was indeed 'the opium of the people' it brought them at least a weekly inoculation against drabness and the sense of comparison, a brief happiness that was not synthetic. For our Congregationalist sample we went to the City Temple, where there was no pulpit but a kind of raised octagonal stage, with a carpeted floor, where the women in the choir wore mortar-board caps, and where at that time the preacher was usually Dr Maud Royden, a onetime suffragette who was originally an Anglican but had been appointed a Congregational Assistant Minister. At the vast Central Hall Westminster we squirmed respectfully under the Old Testament oratory of Dr Dinsdale T. Young, who, when he stooped to consult his sermon notes from a distance of two inches, presented to the packed congregation a shiny pink skull with huge white tufts of hair on each side. And we came to rest, in the sense that we went there quite often, at Kingsway Hall, the Headquarters of the Methodist West London Mission, then presided over by the Revd Ernest J. Rattenbury, a man of incredible and urgent fluency whose mouth and chin seemed always wet with exertion and enthusiasm. He 'packed 'em in' with fiery and superbly pontifical sermons (well advertised in advance) rebuking eminent sceptics like H. G. Wells, Bertrand Russell, and Bernard Shaw.

And in fact it was to Kingsway Hall that my parents now elected to go. After perhaps eighteen months, one evening my parents, yielding to Mr Rattenbury's entreaties from the plat-form, decided to attend the adjacent 'open-air service' which always followed Sunday evening worship in Kingsway Hall. In the absence of a Donald Soper, an open-air religious meeting in a London street is a sad, introvert, and embarrassing business. It has always seemed to me to attract absolutely no serious atten-tion, only derision or hurrying uneasiness. Charles Booth wrote in his *Notebooks*:

One Sunday evening I came across a corps of the Salvation Army, with brass instruments and white helmets for the bandsmen, and the women and officers in regulation dress. They were 30 or 40 in all and capable of producing a prodigious noise as they marched along with a following of ragged children to a street corner, where they formed up and held a rather emotional service, attracting absolutely no attention.

That Kingsway Hall open-air meeting brought the exploration to a close. Harry Woolsey wasn't there, but while I was telling him about it afterwards we both realized that what we had been seeking was some kind of cloistered religious ceremony, attended only by those who wanted it. And yet probably every religion, if it believed in itself, should go out into the streets and try to gain adherents. Certainly a Christian who believed in hell-fire and damnation for non-members should spend every available moment in missionary rescue-work. I am not sure, but I believe that Harry never again attended a religious service.

I did, because my parents did, alternating between Kingsway Hall and the City Temple. I would have been unlikely to sit at home reading while they (and my brothers) went to Sunday evening service; and for this there was the special reason that German bombers were coming over with disturbing frequency and there was an unspoken, but perfectly genuine, feeling in all our minds that, if our number was up, the family would prefer to 'go together'. I clearly remember that this gave chapel-going a special quality (not very clearly defined) of defiance and dyna-mism in which one was 'daring to be a Christian'. The feeling was encouraged by the fact that my father, before setting out, always had to leave word as to where he could be found in the event of an air raid. So far as I was concerned it didn't last, and by the time I was seventeen I was thinking myself into a pagan period which was to last fifty years.

And this process reflected, essentially, one of the unrecorded failures of the Ethical Movement. My brother Harold and I at this period had got interested in the attractions of the South Place Ethical Society, mainly because he was now regularly reading (and expounding to me) the views of John Middleton Murry. Later we heard Middleton Murry deliver at South Place and at the Guildhouse, Eccleston Square, addresses whose purport I have totally and I believe uncharacteristically forgotten. I remember only that the congregation at the Guildhouse sang, to the Welsh melody St. Denio, the hymn:

> Immortal, invisible, God only wise,
> In light inaccessible hid from our eyes,
> Most blessed, most glorious, the Ancient of Days,
> Almighty, victorious, thy great name we praise.

I believe they wouldn't sing that now, the invisible God being in the process of exorcism from the Ethical Societies' hagiology. But they sang it then, with a kind of cerebral fervour. We were much attracted at the time, though it wasn't long before Harold was speaking of its 'fake religiosity' and comparing it with the 'roast turkey' which some vegetarians construct out of nut rissole mixture at Christmas time. My loyalty to the Ethical Movement outlasted his, no doubt because the war took him away from home, and I was warmed by the declared objects of the London Ethical Societies—of which at that time there were four or five. Their main concern was, and I believe still is:

to promote by all lawful means the study of ethical principles; to advocate a religion of human fellowship and service, based upon the principle that the supreme aim of religion is the love of goodness, and that moral ideas and the moral life are independent of beliefs as to the ultimate nature of things and a life after death; and by purely human and natural means to help him to love, know and do the right in all relations of life.

Of course I thought this was tremendous. And it had, or came to have, the open and declared support of such giants as J. A. Hobson, L. T. Hobhouse, Graham Wallas, Gilbert Murray, G. P. Gooch, H. N. Brailsford, and Sir Richard Gregory. As might be expected of a boy who reads too much with a deficiency of understanding, I was always overborne by the illustriousness of such names. Reading took the place of thinking. I saw a blistering attack on 'Ethical Ethermongers' from the vitriolic pen of another of my heroes, J. B. S. Haldane; and then, years later, this attack on *him* by H. G. Wells: 'When other men lie awake in the small hours and experience self-knowledge, remorse and the harsher aspects of life, Haldane I am sure communes quite seriously with that bladder of nothingness, The Absolute, until he falls asleep again.' They were all pagan gods to me at the time, and some of them I was destined to meet in later years. For Harold, and therefore for me, they and their Ethical Societies had made an intelligible and *wholly* acceptable religion from the idea expressed in Tennyson's *Idylls of the King*, which Harold once told me (very privately) that he would like to have as an epitaph:

> It was my duty to have loved the highest:
> It surely was my profit had I known.
> It would have been my pleasure had I seen
> We needs must love the highest when we see it.

The South Place Ethical Society (which didn't build its famous Conway Hall until 1929) was to discover in 1963 that the law did not regard its principles and practice as amounting to a religion; and its premises were refused registration as 'places of worship' within the meaning of the Places of Worship Registration Act 1855 because their members did not worship, revere, or venerate a Supreme Being. Harold and I certainly supposed, in 1917, that they did; which may well illustrate the extent to which we truly understood what was going on at their meetings.

In August 1916 Harold had attested for military service under the Lord Derby Scheme, and thenceforth he proudly wore his khaki armlet with 'GR' on it. Nine months later he was a very proud member of the Honourable Artillery Company, 'the oldest regiment in the British Army'. By September 1917 he was in France, and my heart and my *alter ego* went with him. The occasion of his departure for France remains in my memory indelibly, distressing me to this day. On 31 July General Haig had launched the third battle of Ypres, which came to be known (from its final phase) as Passchendaele. The struggle went on all through August, September, and October, with the loss of hundreds of thousands of young men, a high proportion of them literally drowned in mud. The exact figures have never become known, each new official version being challenged on differing statistical grounds. But the daily lists of casualties in the English newspapers were simply staggering. In those three Passchendaele months the British advanced four miles, forcing a salient in the German lines which, in March the next year when the Germans took the offensive, we evacuated without a fight. My father knew only too well that anyone 'going up the line' at that time stood a poor chance of surviving, and when Harold said goodbye I was severely shaken to see my father embrace him in tears. Just as though they were both foreigners.

I hurried over London Bridge with this soldier brother whom, I now realized for the first time, I should probably not see again. It was my privilege, I felt, to see him off at London Bridge Station for Blackheath, where he was to be billeted at Belmont Hill.

He got no farther than Étaples. The huge proportion of officers being killed (of second lieutenants, it was said, three out of four in their first six months) had led to a frantic intensification of Officers' Training Courses. Every man who remotely resembled 'officer material' was sent back to England to be made into an officer and shipped to France again as a second lieutenant within a matter of weeks. Harold trained at Fleet, in Hampshire, and came home several times in his smart new uniform with a cadet's white band round his peaked cap. I yearned with envy as I contemplated his fine serge khaki tunic, his wide Bedford cord breeches, his soft leather boots. All too soon he left for St. Omer. He was one of those who survived.

Until that time, the Kaiser's War was not a 'total' war or a 'people's war' in the sense that Hitler's was. In the Kaiser's War until 1917 there was an unmistakable 'Upstairs Downstairs' boundary between the participants from the classes. There were eccentrics from Upstairs who joined the ranks, but no one from Downstairs could join anything else. 'Other ranks' who, in the end, became officers were seldom allowed to feel that they belonged in the officer class, and for quite a long time they could have had no difficulty in understanding that their eleva-tion was due to the fearful slaughter going on in the Flanders mud. Five years after the events I speak of here, I myself was in the Police Service hearing the war stories of hundreds of young men bemedalled in the Great War. (I was always miser-ably ashamed of my ribbonless uniform jacket: it was like the odd nakedness of a Freudian nightmare in which the fact that no one notices your nudity seems only to make it worse.) And it was all too obvious that a high proportion of them had been, as they said themselves, 'Gor-Blimey Officers'.

For a couple of years Harold and I had not really been companions, for we had reached the ages at which that had become too difficult; but he remained a much-admired elder brother and I aped his manners and (even to myself) professed his views and interests. His departure for France therefore intensified an already growing sense of loneliness, though this was not a sad state. I was not in the least sorry for myself. My condition was quite different from that of other youths and of the companions I had known in Fulham, because I simply hadn't the money for frequent fares to Fulham. I some-times walked there—it was only six miles—and back again in an evening, and this again was a process that helped to nourish the odd-man-out status which, truth to tell, I was trying hard to enjoy. The time came when the very names of the Under-ground stations I had grown up with were all changed. Walham Green Station became Fulham Broadway, because the Fulham Chamber of Commerce complained that none of the six tube

stations serving Fulham bore its name. And at Walham Green
Station, whose entrance was also for some odd reason the
entrance to the Blue Hall Cinema, that splendid home of the
'moving picture' became the Hibernian Club; while the Red
Hall (the 'fleapit') opposite, after a period as the Walham Green
Gaumont, became a bingo hall.

It was with a mixture of envy and rejection that, in the City
at midday on Saturdays, I observed the various week-end groupings of young people—cricket clubs boarding buses for 'away'
games in unknown places, roller-skating parties bound for some
indoor rink with their skates hanging on straps round their
necks, rambling clubs with maps and Brownie cameras, huge
companies of cyclists in the cycling clubs which came through
the City, riding in perfect formation three abreast and sometimes 250 at a time. I believe I got nearest to pure envy about
the cyclists. How remote in time they now seem.

*

The pound now stood at six US dollars, and it had been seven
ever since the American Civil War. There was as yet no food
rationing, except 'by the purse'. My father's pay was now eight
shining brand-new sovereigns every Friday, straight from the
Bank of England. No one talked about inflation or, as in hum-
bler circles today, 'The Inflation'. They said, 'Things is getting
dearer every week'; and they were. My father had always
spoken of the period just before my babyhood as The Great
Depression, when (speaking relatively) 'the rich groaned and the
poor prospered' and the pound would buy more than it had
ever done since the Napoleonic Wars—a man could keep a
family on a pound a week, *and* somehow save for a seaside
holiday.

I now found myself doing much more of the household
shopping than I had ever done at Fulham, because my father
thought the City streets and traffic were not safe for my
mother, who thought they were but was docile about such
matters. I think she probably smothered even the mortification
she may have felt when Grandma Hewitt, now living permanently

with us, went out on her own at the age of seventy-five plus to draw her pension at Cannon Street Post Office. Patronized because they were within easy walking distance were a greengrover's in Billingsgate; and a Hudson's, a Barham & Marriage's, a Boote & Davis, and a Home and Colonial Stores (all in Cannon Street) for groceries. These smart City grocers, patronized by large numbers of hurrying businessmen on their way home via Cannon Street Station, would still weigh out tea and sugar by hand, making conical sugar bags from strong blue paper; and they still knocked a pound of butter into shape with wooden patters. When I went shopping for my mother, I preferred the Home and Colonial Stores because it reminded me of Finsbury Park. It had been at the Finsbury Park shop where, at the age of eight, I was proudly buying half a pound of fresh butter when the white-coated man behind the counter enquired kindly, '*Best* fresh?' I thought this couldn't be right, and that even if it might be I had better err on the side of thrift on this occasion at least. 'No, no, *worst* fresh,' I said confidently. The story got to my mother's ears, I was made to feel that I had said something extremely witty (though I never understood why), and always thereafter asked in that shop for 'Worst fresh butter please', just to see them all laugh. One of those grocers in Cannon Street, I forget which, even sold beef dripping in tied-up pudding basins; but it could never, surely, have approached the beauty of the beef dripping which my father had always been able to bring home from the police mess kitchens—and which we were now getting even more regularly. Anyone who doesn't know the taste of good beef dripping (especially on toast) will be wasting any sympathy he may have for those who couldn't get butter and *could* get dripping in either of the world wars.

There was a baker called Masons in Sise Lane which my father remembered from forty years earlier, when, according to him, its effect on the salivary juices in the early morning atmosphere of the City was torture if you were hungry and luxurious if you were not. In the lean years of which I am now writing, however, all the bakeries were required by law to produce 'standard bread', the like of which, thank God, I have never seen, smelled, or tasted since. It was like processed sawdust and potato, and even had the taste of warmed-up boiled potato once to be found in cheap seaside boarding houses.

But by late 1916 there were queues for many things, especially lemons, oranges, bananas, potatoes, and apples; and later for eggs and all kinds of meat, bacon, jam, and syrup—for which you had to take your own jar, jug, or tin. I had never before seen people queueing outside shops, though the queueing habit was familiar enough at booking offices of all kinds, and outside theatres and football grounds. The idea began to take hold, in the conversations I heard, that the queue was an orderly and essentially British habit, and that because it suggested a sheep-like docility we had uneasily imported a foreign word to describe it. Indeed I believed this for a long time, and considered it strengthened when, on my first visit to Paris after the Kaiser's War, I saw the French citizenry fighting each other with knees, elbows, handbags, and umbrellas to board their buses, trams, and Métro. Yet in Carlyle's *French Revolution* there appears a reference to 'that talent of spontaneously standing in queue which distinguishes the French people'. By the time I came to see them, they seemed no longer to be distinguished by this custom and we had taken it over. And towards the end of the war, the mere sight in England of a shop-door queue was enough to start a second queue to find out what the first was waiting for.

Food rationing in general did not begin until July 1918, when the war had but four more months to run (meat and butter had been rationed in London since 1 March). With the knowledge that we all have now, I find this fact of history quite inexplicable, except on the possible ground that in order to ration a commodity you must be confident that there will be some to ration. It is also possible, of course, that in 1918 food rationing was the official response to an outbreak of panic buying—suddenly there were huge queues everywhere for things that were not really in short supply; and it seems that consumption now actually increased because every citizen was drawing his full ration, which he hadn't bothered to do before. Rationing equals desirability. But there was a general awareness, I remember, that the Germans were sinking our merchant ships in frightening numbers, and the knowledge was nourishing a recrudescence of the kind of hate which had smashed bakers' windows in 1914, never far below the surface and always ready to erupt.

To me, the sinking of a great ship, indeed of any ship, is such a tragic thing that the hatred this time was totally understandable. When the Germans had torpedoed and sunk the Cunard liner *Lusitania* in 1915, drowning or killing 1,200 people, there were ferocious anti-German riots in the East End of London and in Liverpool. We did not know (as we do now) that on that journey from New York to Liverpool the *Lusitania* was carrying munitions as well as passengers. Nor, I suppose, did most of the passengers. The Germans did, and they struck a medal to commemorate their triumph. I have before me as I write a replica of this medal, issued in London in 1916 by the *Lusitania* Souvenir Medal Committee of No. 32 Duke Street, London, and sold at the time for the benefit of the St. Dunstan's Blinded Soldiers' and Sailors' Hostel. Its accompanying certificate explains that under the legend Keine Bannware (no contraband) the design shows the sinking *Lusitania* bristling with guns and loaded with aeroplanes—'which, as was certified by U.S. Government officials after inspection, the Lusitania did *not* carry', but 'conveniently omits to put in the women and children, which the world knows she *did* carry'. On one side of the medal, under the legend Business Above All (Geschäft über Alles), the figure of Death sits at the Cunard booking office giving out tickets to passengers, in defiance of a German naval officer warning them against submarines. Someone must have known the truth even then, but no doubt the charade had its propaganda value.

And it was all very bewildering to the left-wing, instinctively pacifist feelings which Harold and I had (rather secretly) come to share. When he went to France in 1917 Doris asked him to write something in her autograph album, and left it with him for a day or two. After such an agony of selection as only he was capable of, he steeled himself to write on one of its delicately tinted pages the Divine Quandary just discovered by G. Lowes Dickinson:

> God heard the embattled nations sing and shout
> Gott strafe England and God Save the King,
> God this, God that, and God the other thing.
> Good God! said God, I've got my work cut out.

How would that do, he asked me? It seemed to me that he could hardly have lighted upon anything less suitable for his purpose, or Doris's. If he wanted, I said, to install himself in the bughouse for an indeterminate sentence, this was the way to bring it off. After a discussion that I thought would never come to an end, he reluctantly agreed. Instead he wrote, sombrely and weakly:

> Dulce et decorum est pro patria mori.
> (Going to France, 1917.)

At Spreckley's I had a friend called Hickson, a year older than I, who had been impatiently watching the office calendar as it recorded the days preceding his call-up. At last he could say good-bye all round, and another gap in the office staff had to be filled by a man enticed back from retirement. In three days Hickson was able to call upon us in the uniform of the Royal Horse Artillery. He looked magnificent. He was fidgety with pride. He told us excitedly, over and over again, about his regiment's celebrated status as 'The Right of the Line and the Terror of the World'. He had a little black swagger cane which he carried under his arm, but with which he occasionally struck resounding blows against his puttees. When he had gone we all sighed and turned back to our humdrum work. Less than three months later we heard that he was dead.

*

After about a year in the City I realized, quite suddenly, that

my greatest deprivation since leaving Fulham had been the
Saturday nights and Jim Elderkin's Decca portable gramophone. Then one Saturday he was to come from Fulham to
see us, bring his Decca and some 'topping new records we
hadn't heard'. I do not understand how I got through the
week. The gramophone, in due course, looked smaller in our
new surroundings, seemed less of a miracle. Still less miraculous
was the appalling collection of records that dear old Jim
proudly displayed. 'Hearts and Flowers' played by someone's
brass band, 'The Sunshine of your Smile' (cornet solo by
Corporal-Major Somebody), Enrico Caruso singing Tosti's
'Good-bye' and Nevin's 'The Rosary'—I could never stand the
suspense of waiting until Caruso would burst. But there was a
march record by the Band of the French Garde Republicaine—
Louis Ganne's *Le Père La Victoire* and the March of the Regiment du Sambre et Meuse; and another by the Black Diamonds
Band, Kenneth Alford's 'Colonel Bogey' and 'The Great Little
Army', and these, we decided, were fine; and one overture,
just to show that Jim really knew what we liked: Flotow's
Marthe, undoubtedly because it incorporated Thomas Moore's
song 'The Last Rose of Summer'. When the dread moment
came for Jim to take his marvellous instrument back to Fulham,
he sweetened the sorrow of parting by leaving with us a few
catalogues of recorded music.

The next day, a City Sunday, I roamed the silent and deserted
streets window-shopping for a Decca portable gramophone. I
must have one of my very own. It would have to be saved up
for, but before starting to save up it was necessary to see one in
a shop window. Fleet Street, Ludgate Hill, Gamages in Holborn,
Benetfink's in Cheapside, Aldersgate Street, Moorgate—at last
I saw one, in the window of Keith Prowse & Co. in Cheapside,
price £3. 15s. How long would it take (I turned over some coins
in a pocket) to save up *that* much? Well, one must begin. I
would save every possible penny. I had just started smoking,
and was content with nothing less than Spinet cigarettes, which
were oval-ended and cork-tipped, came in flat tins of twenty,
and always had a two-inch square linen reproduction of a 'great

master'. No more of that. No more solitary Saturday bus rides—
No. 13 to Hendon (The Bell), 21 to Sidcup, 25 to Chadwell
Heath, 7 to Wormwood Scrubs, 11 to Shepherds Bush, 22 to
Barnes Common. (On a summer's evening the front seat of a
London bus-top, open to the sky, was an extra-mural education
of a unique kind.) The saving-up process became an obsession,
its slowness unendurable. Word got round among the police
of the City that the Chief Inspector's sixteen-year-old son was
always to be seen with his nose pressed against the Keith
Prowse window in Cheapside. My father began to worry.
Already he regarded me as a potential delinquent. He saw that
I hadn't enough to do or, if I had, wasn't doing it. I do not
believe he had any fear that I should put a brick through Keith
Prowse's window, but he knew that at the office I was handling
petty cash and postage accounts, and he thought my obsession
was getting dangerous. . . . And, perhaps, it would be rather
nice to have a gramophone in the family.

Suddenly one day he announced that we would go and buy
it. He would make up the necessary sum and I need wait no
longer. I set off with him in a state of excitement that was
just about bearable, but would have unhinged the brain if I
had known what was coming. At Keith Prowse it was nearly
closing time, about six o'clock. A salesman approached us and
my father asked me rhetorically what it was I wanted. I pointed
to the Decca portable and he said to the salesman, as if he had
never seen such a thing, 'Are they any good?' The man assured
him that they were the very thing, unless of course you preferred a cabinet model. He began moving towards a majestic
HMV cabinet, on which the price ticket said £28. Halfway there
my father's eye fell upon a 'table cabinet' priced at £7. 10s. It
was of a dark shiny rosewood, and it was to play a dominant
part in our lives from that moment. Would we like to hear a
couple of specimen records on it? We would. From a selection
placed before him on the glass-topped counter my father
selected the *Der Freischütz* overture and Miriam Lycette singing
'Je Suis Titania' from Gounod's opera *Mignon*. The Decca
portable was forgotten. This was a new world. My father

produced the money at once, and then decided to buy some more records: Mark Hambourg playing 'Liebestraüme' and Ravel's 'Jeux d'Eau', Mischa Elman playing 'Souvenir de Moscou', Eugène Ysaye in the Mendelssohn violin concerto. He was just about to arrange for delivery 'in the course of a day or so' when he saw (I suppose) that the rapture was oozing away from my face. I could carry it, I said. I was strong, sixteen years old, and impatient. (It was about the size, though not of course the weight, of a modern 20-inch television set.) The shopman looked doubtful. I picked it up, held it balanced on my outthrust abdomen, and staggered towards the door. I would have carried it to Penzance, Inverness, anywhere rather than let it out of my sight. I had no more than a quarter of a mile to go with it, but the City homegoing rush hour was in full swing and it was a quarter-mile full of hazard. I still think of it as one of the Great Journeys of the World, with consequences and a justification more perceptible than those of Cook, Amundsen, or Scott.

It is difficult now to recall, but surely the quality of those 'acoustic' recordings must have been very poor by comparison with what was to happen in the 1920s and later, when electrical recording and the long-play, microgroove disc brought such astounding changes. But having almost lived inside a gramophone from the middle of the Kaiser's War until today, I have come to appreciate that, once you are presented with a recognizable facsimile of a musical performance, of whatsoever kind, the highly subjective decision as to how close it gets to the original depends entirely upon the effort you will contribute as a listener. Once you have reached, no matter how painfully, that pinnacle of honesty, you can quite happily concede to anyone that a gramophone (or, as they say today, a record player) never gets very close to a Covent Garden or a Festival Hall performance. In my current estimation, it gets full marks for trying.

CLIMAX

There remain two episodes, differing grotesquely in gravity and significance and yet not altogether dissociated, which are at least sufficiently related in my own story to merit a place together: they were the Russian Revolution in 1917 and the English Police Strike of the following year.

Looking now at contemporary records, it is plain enough that few people in this country, either in 1917 or for many years to come, recognized the cosmic importance of the Russian Revolution. There had been so many Russian revolutions. The Czarist regime seemed based on the hope of foreseeing them, the certainty of crushing them, and the need to provoke one every so often for the purpose of crushing it. The last one remembered by my elders and betters had been in 1905, when the Russians were being soundly beaten in the Russo-Japanese War and the revolutionaries 'stabbed their comrades in the back'. I find it inexplicable, unless it is a trick of age, that I can remember grown-ups discussing the 1905 one but recall no mention of the 1917 one. We knew that the Czar was Nicholas II, cousin of King George V, and that he had been forced by the 1905 Revolution to allow the setting up of a sort of parliamentary assembly called the Duma. Nevertheless, soon after the Kaiser's War began he appointed himself Commander-in-Chief of all the Russian armed forces, leaving the government of the country to his Empress Alexandra (or, in other words, to Rasputin, until that unsavoury priest was shot in 1915). As soon as the Revolution began in February the Czar abdicated, to be shot later with all his family by the revolutionary police; he was succeeded by a Ministry headed by Prince Lvov and Alexander Kerensky, a revolutionary lawyer immensely popular as a defender of political victims.

But during 1917 these events were overshadowed in this country, or at least among my friends and relatives, by America's long-awaited declaration of war on Germany, by mutinies in the French Army, by bread rationing in England, and (in November) by Lenin becoming Russian Chief Commissar and appointing Trotsky his premier. Whenever my brother Harold was home on leave, he and I discussed these events with some excitement and little understanding. The Russians would now wipe out the German forces, he told me, because henceforth they would fight as idealists. Instead the new Russian High Command proposed an immediate peace, with 'no annexations, no indemnities'. Ah well, we said, the only kind of peace that would not 'sow the dragon's teeth'.

Nor are there many English histories of the Kaiser's War from which you would gather that what was slowly coming to fruition in that vast country was the most sickening mass cruelty the world had ever seen. Certainly the only communist I knew, a jovial middle-aged packer in the dispatch room at Spreckley's, told us all repeatedly, glibly, and happily that it was through Russia's new government that the war would now be brought quickly to an end, agreement being reached by the European peoples in defiance of their inept and bloodthirsty rulers, who would all be deposed. I made the mistake of repeating some of this at home, at a time when there was much anxiety about a growing wave of unrest in the police service. My domestic status slumped badly once again and I took refuge in silence and solitary speculation.

Harold and I had a political idol in the person of Mr Arthur Henderson, who was chairman of the Parliamentary Labour Party and a member of the War Cabinet. In 1917 Lloyd George sent him to Russia, with an urgent mandate to try and deflect the triumphant socialists from their deplorable efforts to end the war. He came back totally converted to the Russian view, and began advocating a full Stockholm Conference of the Socialist International (to include the Germans) and an attempt to bring about peace by direct communication between the workers. The Prime Minister having promptly sacked him, all the newspapers proceeded to vilify him as a traitor. But he had started an anti-war movement in which I took a silent, rather bewildered, and on the whole unhappy interest.

Then in November came the famous letter in the *Daily Telegraph* (*The Times* had turned it down) from the Marquis of Lansdowne, former Liberal Foreign Secretary, saying that the war would destroy civilization and that peace should be sought at once on the basis of a return to the conditions that had existed on 4 August 1914. Actually he had circulated this as a private memorandum to the Asquith Cabinet a year before, while he was Minister without Portfolio; and it was brusquely rejected. The only thing I clearly understood about all this at the time was that among our leading politicians there were good men who thought the war could be brought to an end at once. That was what I wanted now, and I was perplexed and angry that it seemed so dangerous to talk about it. Ours was not a very political household, but the names of Henderson and Lansdowne, absolutely heroic to me, were now included among the words you could not use at mealtimes.

All this while, from our arrival there in February 1916 until the end of the war, I had very little contact with the policemen living at Cloak Lane Station. From the top of the stairs, six floors up and out of bounds to me, there came always the inimitable click of billiard balls, and I longed to get up there and learn to play. My father was adamant in refusing me permission and his reason no doubt seemed good enough. He thought that as the son of the resident Chief Inspector I ought to keep out of the way, giving no grounds for any suspicion that I was 'spying on the men'. As soon as the war was over he relaxed this rule for some reason or other, possibly the general euphoria, or it may even have been that so long as there was danger from enemy aircraft he had preferred not to have me spending my time on top floors anywhere (air raids went on all through 1918). It was not until the end of 1918, accordingly, that I got to know any of the resident single men, and thereafter I spent much time among the twenty or thirty of them who frequented the billiard room. Among these I formed a number of friendships of the quality that could remain undamaged even after I was able to beat them at billiards. (Some of them could retaliate by wiping the floor with me at snooker.) But in 1918 I knew little of the anxiety and resentment which were slowly changing a company of good-natured, leg-pulling comrades into a battalion of malcontents— a receptive audience for the so-called 'peace-at-any-price' internationalists called into the open by the growing anti-war movement.

The top rate of pay for a constable was forty-eight shillings a week, and he was far behind the average wage of an unskilled labourer. His hard-won 'weekly rest day' (made statutory in 1910 after years of campaigning) was withdrawn at the outbreak of war, and in many forces without any compensation. There were big discrepancies in the pay of different forces: Glasgow policemen were getting a pound a week more than London policemen. There had been a Police and Prison Officers Union since 1913, its aims being advertised in the *Police Review* in October 1913 as follows:

To safeguard the police against official tyranny and injustice, to improve the conditions of the police service, to ensure equal chances of promotion, to maintain just and efficient discipline, to purge the service of corrupt and unworthy members, and to secure for the public honest and efficient police administration. Entrance fee one shilling, annual subscription one shilling.

And a further clause constituted 'a permanent guard against any possibility of members withholding their services as a means of obtaining redress', an absolutely specific anti-strike undertaking. On 18 December 1913 Sir Edward Henry, the Commissioner of the Metropolitan Police, issued an order declaring the Union unlawful and promising dismissal for anyone joining it. About 1,000 men nevertheless joined it and, for the time being, most of them kept very quiet. The aims set out above reflect the ideals (I think you can call them no less) of a man named John Syme, who had been dismissed from the Metropolitan Police in 1910 when holding the rank of Inspector. His story is too

long to tell here, but the qualities that brought him into conflict
with his superiors were that he was honest, unbending, fearless,
tactless, Scottish, and Christian. The conflict gradually and
tragically changed him from a conscientious policeman into a
persecuted crank, in and out of prison for breaking Downing
Street windows, for publishing criminal libels, and for threatening to murder people, and carrying a sandwich-board in Whitehall
(where I saw him many times) proclaiming his story in chalked
block capitals too small for anybody to read. It was he who
founded the Police and Prison Officers Union, and his known
eccentricity would have ensured that it got off to a bad start,
even if there had been the smallest chance of its getting off to
a good one.

Even so, the Union had no collective voice to which the
authorities would or could listen. Lacking such a voice, the
police grievances festered and spread; and on the evening of
29 August 1918 large numbers of the Metropolitan night duty
men, due to begin work at 9.45 p.m., either absented themselves or went to their stations to declare that they were on
strike. The next day, with the strike spreading rapidly, the
Home Office offered to negotiate with 'two men from each
Division' (which, if taken up literally, would have confronted
them with about fifty men!) but *not* with the Union as such.
The men's representatives declined this offer and said that if the
Union men were not received 'we will call the City Police out
on strike at six o'clock tonight'. This seems to have been
intended as a kind of trump card, the City Police being mytho-
logized as a body of deep-blue incorruptibles embodying the
Establishment itself. If the City Police would strike, anything
could happen. But the bid failed, and accordingly the strike
call was dispatched to the City Police. Of these, 500 assembled
in front of the Royal Exchange and marched off to Whitehall,
carrying London Trades Council standards, Labour Party
banners, and (seen for the first time) streamers proclaiming the
Police and Prison Officers Union. On the morning of 31 August
1918, on my way from Spreckley's to cash a wages cheque at
the Midland Bank in Threadneedle Street, I watched them go

by. From a distance I saw my worried father, standing in uniform at the corner of Mansion House Place; and I could see
that they bore him no ill-will. As they passed him, the majority
lifted their hats and caps—there was a preponderance of straw
boaters—and once they raised an embarrassed kind of cheer. In
the event, Lloyd George bought them off with a rise of pay
and what they took to be a promise that a 'police union' might
be considered again when the war was won (and in this they
were sadly mistaken). The whole story of the 1918 police strike
is vividly told by Gerald W. Reynolds and Anthony Judge in
The Night the Police Went on Strike,[1] and knowing at least Mr
Judge I am confident that the book as a whole is better researched
and more reliable than appears from the following extract,
which I welcome this opportunity to correct:

As the City Police filed past Clack Lane Police Station [*sic*: the authors
mean Cloak Lane, but the marchers didn't go within 400 yards of Cloak
Lane] they came under the cold, disapproving scrutiny of Chief Inspector
Hewitt [he was much in sympathy with their plight, and sick at heart
rather than disapproving] who was standing stiffly to attention, his schoolboy son by his side. [His only schoolboy son then was Roland, who wasn't
there.] The son . . . better known as C. H. Rolph, recalls many hours of
his boyhood spent in the company of the constables who lived at the
Station, especially one Jack Zollner, the local secretary of the Union, and
it was from them that young Hewitt first began to form his own political
beliefs. [As I have said, I knew few of the men before 1919, when I was
first allowed to use the billiard room. I never discussed political beliefs
with any of them, but gathered from their backchat that, if they voted at
all, they voted Tory because the Tories seemed fondest of them and gave
the least trouble; and I never met Zollner in my life.]

I hope Messrs Reynolds and Judge will forgive me this exercise in putting straight a garbled record based (so far as I
remember) on one telephone conversation, though I would
gladly have done it at the time if I could have seen a proof
of what they proposed to say. I had often heard the name of
P.C. Zollner in my father's references to police events at that
time, and he always contrived to make it sound both German and
Russian (the unholiest of current conjunctions) by pronouncing

---

[1] Weidenfeld & Nicolson, 1968.

it 'Tsolnah'. Reynolds and Judge describe Zollner variously as an ex-Grenadier Guardsman who had been in the retreat from Mons and as an ex-merchant seaman. Perhaps he was both. But by 1921, when I myself arrived in the City Police, he had become a fading legend; he was one of fifty-eight men who had been dismissed from the force in 1919 for organizing and taking part in a second strike (a futile attempt, this, to achieve recognition for the Police and Prison Officers Union). I never knew him; but I have absolutely no doubt that all policemen, both of that time and now, are immensely in his debt.

In fact, the few City policemen I had contact with in those years were all bandsmen, whose concert rehearsals and weekly practices I was still allowed to attend. The City of London Police Band at that time (1916–18) was, I have to recognize, not of the standard it had known when my father was its solo flautist (1895–1908) and when its conductor was Mr Sydney Jones, composer of the then popular musical comedies *The Geisha* and *San Toy*. Sydney Jones was really an orchestral man, but he liked conducting military bands and enjoyed arranging scores for them. He specialized in arrangements of Wagner, in whose music he was so expert and so steeped that he might have been the original for Bernard Shaw's *Perfect Wagnerite*. And he had the special admiration for the City of London Police which, seemingly encountered everywhere in my childhood and adolescence, made me extremely proud of my connection with it. I must not pretend, of course, that its reputation rested solely on the excellence of its military band. It also had a water-polo team, which (until someone invented the Australian crawl) was invincible, a tug-of-war team that could make any other run after it (and was chosen *en bloc* for an Olympic Games entry), a crack rifle team and some leading amateur boxers. It maintained a six-foot minimum height standard, and its members were thoroughly taught (even if they knew already) how to wear a uniform, keep it smart, and look as if they belonged in it.

Those semicircles of shirt-sleeved musicians represented for me a weekly occasion that I longed for to an extent that would

certainly have surprised them all. I can see them all now, and
the odd shapes that their faces assumed in the stress of performance: palpitating cheeks for the euphoniums, horns,
trombones and tuba, pursed lips for clarinets, oboes and bas-
soons, distorted little *embouchures* for flute and piccolo, and
a general tendency to turn red in allegro passages and purple
in fortissimo. 'Nice blow this evening,' they would say to
each other as they packed their instruments into their black
cases, and they were always right. In 1916 they had an exceptionally fine tenor trombone, a splendid solo cornet, and a
clarinettist (later to be a detective superintendent) who would
never, in a perfect world, have been allowed to do anything
but play Mozart, Weber, Auber, and Rossini. They also had a
horn player who was so awful that in public performances his
part was always 'doubled' by some other, and louder, instrument. But they were a fine lot, all touched by a little of the
magic which, for me, hovers about the presence of any musician,
and all extremely tolerant and friendly towards myself. These
men, however, did nothing to 'form my political views', certainly not left-wing ones. Policemen then almost certainly
voted Tory if they voted at all—and there was a strong belief
among many policemen, I found, that they were still not
entitled to vote at all, though that disability had been removed
by Act of Parliament in 1893; and they were still in the after-
light of that period when it was an act of some daring, among
the working classes, even to vote Liberal.

Otherwise, war or no war, things went along much as they
always had, except that a great many people seemed to think
that they were ill. I am prepared to believe that it was in those
years that someone first said 'There's a lot of it about'. And an
examination of some contemporary magazines revives my own
impression that patent medicine advertisements were then at
their lying zenith, probably because of war neurosis and all the
ills that flowed from it. The world-wide influenza epidemic of
1917–18 had probably made us a nation, if not of hypochon-
driacs, then of mutual diagnosticians. In England alone, during
the winter of 1918, there were 150,000 deaths from this strange

and terrifying virus. The deaths in India amounted to 16 million.
No one in my family escaped the disease and indeed I believe
more than half the population of Great Britain caught it.
With tragic irony, multitudes of British servicemen died of
influenza within a few days before or after the Armistice.

On my long weekend walks from the City, to say nothing of
the longer (but rarer) bus-rides, the familiar milestones were
famous advertisements on hoardings and buildings which never
changed and which, indeed, had the permanence of being
enamelled in bright colours on huge sheets of metal. They all
extolled cure-all medicines and skin-care preparations, and
were identical with those to be seen among ladies' fashion advertisements in the newspapers, where the cylinder-shaped women
of the time, always depicted with very small and only just
visible feet splayed out like birds' claws, peeped at the world
from under their awful tight-fitting cloche hats. Wells's *Tono
Bungay* was in no sense an exaggeration. There was news for
the bald-headed that Nuda Veritas 'Causes a Luxuriant Growth'
and that Harlene 'Produces Luxuriant Hair'. Brown's Bronchial
Troches were boldly (and then of course quite legally) alleged
to 'cure cough, cold, hoarseness and influenza'; hooping cough
(*sic*: this was how we spelled whooping in those days) called for
Roche's Herbal Embrocation, which in addition 'cured Bron-
chitis, Lumbago and Rheumatism'. Any kind of embrocation
for whooping cough must have seemed an advance on the long-
established custom of taking children round to the gasworks
and carrying or wheeling them about in prams while they
inhaled and were induced to vomit by the fumes. (Some
mothers did this day after day for weeks, the children strained
horribly in their attempts to vomit, and I don't doubt that this
had much to do with the high proportion of cross-eyed children among my contemporaries.)

We were exhorted to Keep Zam Buk Handy and Rub It In
for the cure of almost anything. A housewife with one hand
pressed into the small of her back reminded us that Every
Picture Tells a Story, and that the Story could be given a happy
ending by Doan's Backache Kidney Pills. There were Dr Maurice

Brown's Chlorodyne and Dr Williams's Pink Pills for Pale People, both claiming to cure the same things. Pears Soap (with no apostrophe) was 'Matchless for the Complexion', while Mellin's Food (which did have an apostrophe) proclaimed that 'Thousands of weakly children whose lives were despaired of have been restored by Mellin's Food to vigorous health'. And two of the most widely advertised remedies, Scott's Emulsion and anyone's cod-liver oil and malt, constantly reminded me that a supply of these was nearly always in the house, ineffectually concealed in different places because I, and I believe I alone, loved them both so much that I would seize any opportunity to steal a spoonful. Today I learn that both these products were (and, I suppose, are) detested by all right-minded children, a discovery which has made this revelation the more embarrassing and soul-baring.

A highly evocative advertisement I have come across recently (it was in *The Times* of 25 October 1918) affords an indication that, in whatever period, respectable erotic titillation will go as far as it safely can. An immensely popular author at the time (much read by my parents) was William le Queux, turning out several predictably short-lived novels a year and succeeding because he could always 'tell a good yarn'. In the early part of the century his book *The Invasion of 1910*, which foretold the Kaiser's War but got it all wrong, frightened some people almost as much as Orson Welles's radio version of the H. G. Wells book *The War of the Worlds* did in 1938. Le Queux wrote often as a doctor, which gave him decent scope for respectable titillation—'many a woman has sniggered provocatively as I have placed my stethoscope upon her bared breast'. *The Times* advertisement announced the forthcoming publication, by John Long, of *The Love Intrigues of the Kaiser's Sons* by William Le Queux. 'The author', promised *The Times*, 'lifts the veil from the private lives of the Kaiser's sons, showing how despite the iron hand of Prussian discipline they were frequently involved in affairs of the heart with girls in all classes of society.' Much like the sons of other bigwigs, in fact, but eligible for remunerative exposure because their father was The Enemy and the girls ought to have been protected by what we were all fighting to destroy, the iron hand of Prussian discipline.

Less exotic advertisements caught my eye at the same time. 3 October 1918: 'Jam may shortly be rationed—register now at Lipton's.' 9 October: 'Jam, marmalade, syrup, treacle and honey are to be rationed from November 3—use the red coupons on LEAF FIVE, marked SPARE.' 'It is anticipated that it may be necessary to ration paraffin oil and candles—though there may be exemptions for nursery nightlights.' But the war was about to end with what, presumably, must have been dramatic suddenness for our leaders, who were just getting down to it. On 8 October, for example, there was Mr Winston Churchill, Minister of Munitions, telling a meeting of munitions workers at Glasgow that 'Victory *may* come next year—I cannot say that I am over sanguine'. And on 10 October the Food Controller announced, once again, that it was 'everyone's duty to eat as little bread as possible, to save shipping space for the American soldiers coming over'.

'None of us will live to see the end of this war,' said Lord Northcliffe in September 1918, which must have sounded a bit grim to my generation. Happily a few days later Ludendorff, the German Supreme Commander, told his Government that they must seek an armistice at once. He wanted 'peace at any price', without waiting for the Allies to draw up peace terms; and the plan suggested by President Wilson as early as January 1917 (his famous Fourteen Points) was now found acceptable.

At home we found it simply unbelievable. For most of us the word 'Armistice' came into the language for the first time. Many people pronounced it as though it were some kind of ice, and some called it 'The Armistrice'. It was something the enemy had to sign when you had beaten him, it put him on bail while the full details of his sentence were being worked out. The Kaiser had fled to Holland, announced his abdication, and for some time faced the prospect of trial in London as a war criminal. But he died in his bed at Doorn Castle in 1941, with his invading countrymen once again around him. On the very day of his flight, 9 November, Germany announced that it had become a republic; and at five o'clock on the morning of 11 November, Armistice Day, a German delegation signed an armistice which came into force at 11 a.m. In spite of which, and as a kind of commentary on the communications system of the period, for a week or two men went on killing each other in distant parts of the world, bombing towns and sinking ships and spreading misery as though by mechanical momentum. At last, with the exception of sailors who were to die as their ships struck mines (a mine in the Baltic, for example, sank HMS *Cassandra* with all hands on 4 December), it was all over. And we all went mad.

We had been told that the great news would be announced that Monday morning at 11 o'clock by the firing of maroons, which we had so long accepted as air raid warnings. It was ten past eleven when they went off in the City. Mr Edwards, our venerable cashier in the counting house at Spreckley's, flung down his pen impatiently and made for the basement. No, no, we called after him, this is not an air raid, this must be *peace*. But he had gone and, in the ensuing frenzy, he was forgotten. We all crowded into the big Cloth Department, which had huge ground-floor windows looking out on to Cannon Street. People from the five upper floors came running down the fine carpeted stairway at the back of the Department; men and girls from the Furs, the Mantles, the Skirts and Costumes, the Children's. Frock-coated men and shirt-sleeved juniors and immaculate saleswomen and beautiful models, all calling out incoherently and twittering and (incredible in those austere premises) actually embracing and kissing. Two or three people ran down the short flight of steps from the swing doors into the street, and then everybody followed, the building emptied as if someone had shouted 'Fire!' Work was over for the day, by informal mass resolution.

In Cannon Street a man on a bicycle was broken-windedly blowing the All Clear with a bugle he could hardly control as his cycle wobbled through the growing crowds. For some reason, we all moved towards the Royal Exchange and the Mansion House, the very centre of the City where stands also,

immemorially, the Bank of England. At the Royal Exchange
someone had run up the Union Jack, and a stiff breeze filled
it out. The Royal Exchange steps were black with people.
Queen Victoria's statue was covered with clingers-on. Buses
were accumulating in all the streets converging on the Royal
Exchange, because the dense crowds had slowed them to the
pace of the general movement, and eventually they all had to
stop. They were all empty inside. Everyone was on top, far too
many for safety. People were standing and sitting on the canopy
over the driver's seat. One bus, a No. 11, was marked in chalk
FREE TO BERLIN and was cheered madly by everyone. Men
and women had taken off their boots and shoes so that they
could bang them against the metal advertisement sheets on
the buses' sides: anything, everything that could make a noise.
Electric motor horns (called Klaxons from the manufacturer's
name) were still quite a new thing—the majority of motorists
still used a 'Harry Tate', squeezing air from a rubber ball into
a brass trumpet—and now they were snorting everywhere; a
truly horrible cacophony made bearable, made even exciting,
by its otherwise incommunicable message of triumph, relief,
and happiness.

Hundreds of sellers of small flags appeared from nowhere.
Where did they get all those little flags so suddenly? I remembered the Boat Race badges, cadged from their wearers once the
race was over—for sale as new the following year. But these
little flags couldn't have been in store since the Boer War or
Mafeking Night. The astute London street traders had seen
all this coming and had put their money on Peace. Individual
buyers bought dozens and dozens of them, sticking them into
every button-hole and other parts of their clothing and all over
their hats. Flags of every conceivable kind, including some that
looked so home-made as to be unlikely flags from anywhere.
The flag of any one of the Allies was as good as that of any
other. Huge military lorries came from nowhere crammed with
standing and cheering civilians. Then down came the rain, and
no one cared a damn. Piano-organs appeared and people danced
in the roads—the one adequate way, it seemed, in which to

express excited joy and otherwise inexpressible relief. Those who couldn't dance rang handbells, banged trays, adding to the din of the Klaxons, the screaming whistles, anything and everything that could bellow, echo, vibrate, or shrill.

At last I reached Mappin and Webb's Corner, to find that a crowd later estimated at 100,000 people, crammed into the converging thoroughfares from every direction, had gradually stopped making a noise as the Lord Mayor, on the steps of his Mansion House, seemed anxious to say something to them. Inaudibly from where I stood, he said a few words that brought fresh cheers and tears, and then led three thunderous cheers for the King, followed by three more each for the Army and the Navy. And when he (or someone) began singing the Old Hundredth, it was gradually taken up by the thousands of rain-soaked revellers in the mightiest quasi-musical roar I have ever heard; and I was astounded that everyone near me seemed to know the words. Everyone seemed also able to sing them with gusto—always a surprise to me on such an occasion, for under such emotion I can never produce a sound, the larynx having gone off duty until everything gets back to normal:

Praise God from whom all blessings flow,
Praise him all creatures here below;
Praise him above, ye heavenly host,
Praise Father, Son, and Holy Ghost.

It was a colossal sound, frightening, isolating; it was as though the God of Thunder himself had taken possession of that mysterious entity by which any crowd exceeds the sum of its constituent members. The very road and buildings seemed to shake with it. It's a hymn with only one verse, but what comparable crowd could sing it today? Everyone can sing the inane first verse of the National Anthem, which people tolerate because they can sing it without the brain getting in the way. But what a magnificent National Anthem the Old Hundredth would make!

Then across by the corner of Princes Street I saw Grace Jessett, our pretty red-headed telephonist from Spreckley's. I shall now disclose that I was temporarily potty about Grace Jessett, who was about ten years older than I, looked about the same age, and behaved as if she were much younger. She allowed me to be potty about her because it was amusing and (by contrast with my own condition) caused her no loss of sleep or appetite. I pushed and thrust my way towards her, effecting, I remember, some brief changes of expression on the rapt faces of revellers. Within a few minutes my arm was around her waist (it had never been there before) and I was asking tenderly why she was crying. Then for the first time I noticed that nearly everyone was either crying or mopping up. Why was I not crying? It is something about myself that I have never understood, that I cannot be of a crowd; cannot cheer, hoot or boo, or publicly rejoice or mourn. I have often watched, furtively and fascinated, the cheerers, hooters and booers, watched the chords stand out in their necks and the eyes in their sockets. These, I have told myself, are the natural and generous people. When required or expected to cheer as one of a crowd, even under discipline, I've always opened my mouth and mimed, but no sound has ever emerged. Am I alone? I've left it a bit late to find out.

Grace said she would like to go to St. Paul's Cathedral. So would I, then. Hand in hand we made our way down Princes Street and along the less crowded Gresham Street to St. Paul's. The Churchyard, when we got to it, was as crammed as the Mansion House crossing. It took fifteen minutes to get round to the west doors of the Cathedral, for the moment the only way in—only one small door was open. A policeman told us the Cathedral was 'packed to the doors', and that this was for the second time since one o'clock, but he allowed us to squeeze in and stand flattened against the door. The silence in that vast and lofty auditorium, where thousands of people stood motionless, was as shattering as the uproar still going on outside; and then, gradually, you could hear the faint distant echoing sound, as your ears began to come open again, of a service going on at the eastern end, 200 yards away.

As a stimulus to the right kind of thinking, this was more

effective. I found myself wondering what was happening in other cities, in Birmingham, Manchester, Liverpool—and then Paris and New York; and then Berlin? What were the defeated Germans doing? Years later I learned from German friends that they, too, were waving flags, singing, and dancing in the streets. Did it matter, then, who had won? Everybody had won, everybody had lost. We British had celebrated our shattering defeat at Mons and the nightmare retreat that followed by giving every single participant a medal. Mr Herbert had often told me of an American essayist, Elbert Hubbard, who went down in the *Lusitania* when she was torpedoed in 1915, and of how he had said 'God will not look you over for medals, degrees, or diplomas: He will look for scars.'

All was quiet again next morning. At Spreckley's we were all back at work, and so it seemed was every firm we did business with. One of my elderly counting-house colleagues came late with a hangover: that was all. I have heard it said that the London revelling went on for three days and nights. It did not. Some historians seem to have been persuaded, perhaps by colourful newspaper files, that the public convulsions almost rivalled the Gordon Riots. Even the impish Mr A. J. P. Taylor has been allowed to enshrine for ever in the Oxford History of England (*English History 1914–1945*, page 114) this astonishing glimpse of a saturnalia that never took place:

Total strangers copulated in doorways and on the pavements. They were asserting the triumph of life over death. The celebrations ran on with increasing wildness for three days, when the police finally intervened and restored order.

I believe I should have noticed some of this, especially what was happening on the wet London pavements. I was there. The idea that the police 'restored order' when they judged, after three orgiastic days, that the happy citizenry had better get on with its work, is comic but not original, giving aid to the process by which, even if history does not repeat itself, historians will go on repeating each other.

But on 11 November 1918 we survivors did have a corporate

sense of history, of having lived together through Armageddon. I had just completed my seventeenth year and was convinced that world peace, and all the happiness to which it was essential, now lay before us all and stretched to infinity. In England at the age of seventeen your adolescence comes to a statutory end. No longer a juvenile in the eyes of the law, fully responsible accordingly for all your misdeeds, you are thrust into manhood by tribal custom. For this emancipation I had long been benevolently prepared by my father, but I had never supposed that my state of protected youth would end, or my manhood begin, with the gigantic Allelujah in which I had just participated. My appetite for an exciting future had been whetted, throughout the war, by my father's assurances not only that the lights would all come on again in the streets, that nights would no longer be disturbed by danger, that decent bread and real butter would again be plentiful, but that (far above all) the bands and orchestras I had so sorely missed would be playing everywhere.

So the twentieth century and myself set off boldly into the mercifully unknown, myself keeping prudently a few months behind.